PRAISE

Remembering Who I Am

"*Remembering Who I Am* is a guidebook for anyone who's ever questioned their worth or purpose in life. It offers step-by-step, practical wisdom that will lead you back to the source of power and love. You will want to read it over and over again and use it daily for inspiration." **–Dr. Chris Michaels**, author of *The Power of You*

"The human experience we all have undertaken is not always the path filled with fragrant flowers and sunshine. Often it is a road that's pitted and unkempt and full of unseen obstacles. This spiritual guide by Jane Beach offers a refreshing reminder that the 'light at the end of the tunnel' really is there, within reach. Her compassion and understanding show how to regain the joy and happiness that my soul truly is and I feel blessed. I'm so grateful to read this book and 'remember who I am.'" **–Nanette Littlestone**, bestselling author of *F.A.I.T.H.:Finding Answers in the Heart*

"Jane Beach writes with a conscious, applicable aim. Her offerings never fail to send fundamental truths directly to the reader's heart with precision and care. *Remembering Who I Am* is spiritual instruction you can feel instantly and apply constantly. It will reawaken you to your expanded potential." **–David Ault**, author of *The Grass Is Greener Right Here*

"Through experience, daily attention and practical application, Jane Beach reveals one of the foundation principles of life—*Remembering Who I Am*. Her book takes the reader on an epic journey to self-realization and purpose—and they come through remembering."

–Jim Rosemergy, Senior Minister, Unity of Fort Myers, author, international speaker.

"Jane Beach's book, *Remembering Who I Am*, helps us to do just that. Her delightful style is based in a deep connection to her own divinity which helps us explore our individual spiritual paths with grace, beauty and ease. Jane shares from her keen mind and huge heart. Her high consciousness, coupled with her *joie de vivre* make this an exceptional book for anyone interested in introspection and personal growth." –REV. DAVID GOLDBERG, Publisher, Science of Mind Publishing, *Science of Mind Magazine*

"As you read *Remembering Who I Am* you'll discover it really is a guide book—but not necessarily one that shows you the external terrain of life. With profound reverence, eloquence, and wisdom, Jane Beach takes you on the most sacred journey of your life—the journey back to the place you never really left—your oneness with Infinite Presence, where you'll find the precious Self you were *born to be* awaiting your arrival. Remembering who you are isn't a once in a lifetime awakening—it's a way of being, a way of walking a sacred earth *every day* of your life. It's also how you bring the gift you are to the planet. *Remembering Who I Am* is an exquisite guidebook that will take you the distance. The practice is to remember to remember this is the journey you were born to make!"
   –DR. DENNIS MERRITT JONES, Author of *Your (Re)Defining Moments: Becoming Who You Were Born to Be*; and, *The Art of Uncertainty: How to Live in the Mystery of Life and Love It*

"Jane has beautifully crafted an invitation to move into an awareness of our eternal life and the opportunity to remember the truth of our being in every moment. Use this book as a guide to happiness and self-love." –CYNTHIA JAMES, Author, Speaker, Spiritual Coach.

Remembering Who I Am

Remembering

Who I Am

A Spiritual Guide to Happiness

JANE BEACH

KENOS PRESS
an Imprint of Six Degrees Publishing Group
Portland • Oregon • USA

KENOS PRESS FIRST EDITION

KENOS PRESS
an Imprint of Six Degrees Publishing Group
5331 Macadam Avenue, Suite 258
Portland, Oregon 97239

ISBN 978-1-942497-10-3

eBook ISBN: 978-1-942497-11-0

US Library of Congress Control Number:
2015950759

Published in the United States of America

Editorial and Design Supervision: Denise C. Williams

Inquiries: Publisher@SixDegreesPublishing.com

Printed Simultaneously in the United States of America,
the United Kingdom and Australia

1 3 5 7 9 10 8 6 4 2

You yourself, as much as
anybody in the entire universe,
deserve your love and affection.
~ Buddha

Contents

Contents

- Practicing Happiness through Meditation
- Taking Responsibility for My Prosperity
- Owning My Life
- Breaking Out!
- The Power of My Enthusiasm
- Putting Guilt and Shame in Perspective
- In the Middle of the Big Picture

- Love's Divine Attention
- Taking Care of Myself
- Detaching with Love
- Making a Difference
- Loving Kindness is Who I Am
- What Would Love Do Now?
- Personal Liberation
- Boundaries Benefit Everyone
- Faith in Times of Uncertainty
- I Matter in the World
- Everything in My Life is *For* Me
- My Life is My Ministry
- My Own Inner Light

Foreword

Something within us knows that we have forgotten. Since that first night that we wandered out of our cave and stared up into the endless depths of the starry night sky there has been an awareness, an often undefined knowing somewhere deep within us that there is more to this human equation than meets the eye. Like a distant whisper, that still, small but persistent invitation impels us to know more of ourselves, to know our nature, to know our purpose and our design. Something within our collective hearts and souls stirred that night, and has been stirring ever since. Something within us knows there is more, and desperately wants to remember.

It's not by accident that you have picked up this book, that you have been drawn to this author, my friend and teacher Jane Beach. I have had many teachers along the way. And the day came when I was blessed to cross paths with a small but mighty package of Life and Light that is Jane Beach. And my life was forever changed.

Spiritual teachers are, thankfully, different than they once were. Not separate anymore, not preaching to the people from a place on-high, but instead being one with the people, teaching not from a place of theory or rhetoric or from some inherited theology, but instead from the heart, from a place of experience, of gentle knowing, a place of love and compassion. Jane is that kind of teacher.

This book then is not some dense theoretical philosophizing that has no practical application in daily life. Quite the opposite. Jane knows, you see, that spiritual living isn't something "out there". It's not just something that we do for an hour or two a week on Sunday. It's not something that anyone can tell us how to do. It's an invitation to wander into a way of being, a way of seeing life and of showing up in the world. She knows. She is remembering too, and her teachings are a sharing of that remembering of who we are, what we are, and why we are.

I invite you to gently and easily meander through these pages with my colleague, my teacher, my friend Jane. For on those nights when we wander outside and stare up into the starry night sky and something stirs, deep within, it's nice to have a friend like Jane alongside.

May you wander well.

Rev. Jeff Anderson
Senior Minister
Oakland Center for Spiritual Living
Author of *The Nature of Things ~ Navigating Everyday Life with Grace*

Introduction

Choosing happiness in our everyday lives takes courage! If you're tempted to play small in order to appease another, you're shoving happiness away. Bucking the status quo . . . standing up for yourself . . . owning your self-worth . . . can be scary. That's where choice comes in—will you choose your happiness or give it away?

Remembering Who I Am is a gentle reminder that you are worth everything that puts a smile on your face! Your job is to be happy, and let your happiness shine! You don't have to be good enough, smart enough, or talented enough—you already *are* enough, just as you are. This book was written as a guide to help you discover the beauty of your own worth and choose the happiness that Life is offering you.

Learning to appreciate *you* is an honorable goal, one that we will address in this book. You can't know the beauty of your light without first living in darkness; you can't feel your power until you've known powerlessness; you can't appreciate peace until you've dwelled in chaos. The ups and downs of your human-ness leads you right back to the truth and beauty of who you really are. You may have heaped so much fear, guilt and self-judgment on that light that you can't see it in the moment, but it's still there. *Remembering Who I Am* will help you peel back the muck to discover the magnificence that is *you*.

~

There is a Presence . . . a Higher Power . . . the God of your understanding . . . that knows who you are and loves you without reservation, no matter what ugly thoughts exist in your mind or how chaotic your life may be. This book is a reminder that today's a new day, and as you remember who you truly are, including the messiness of your very human life, you will uncover the light that's shining bright as you!

I didn't always feel this way. For the first fifty years of my life I was an atheist. I thought people who believed in any kind of a Higher Power were weaklings, using the idea of God as a crutch to bail them out of situations they couldn't handle on their own. I was pretty arrogant and snippy about it, making fun of people who "believed" or went to church. Little did I know that one day I'd become a minister!

In 1998, at a low point in my life, the Beloved made itself known to me in a way that I couldn't ignore. I went from being that snotty atheist to trusting the presence and power of the greatest Love of all—the God of my understanding—constantly. The instant I recognized that what I was experiencing was what people called God, I knew I had been loved without reservation my whole life and this great Love had just been waiting for me to notice it. My realization was simple, and yet it changed everything.

I know the Presence as energy—that's why I refer to it as "it" instead of him or her. How can energy know me intimately and be warm, comforting and loving? I have no idea—I just know that it does. Its energy is expansive, tender, powerful, and calm all at the same time, gently wrapping its love around me when I need comfort and helping me stay strong enough to move through my old stuff to create the life I have now. I have lots of names for the God of my understanding: the Beloved, Divine Love, the greatest Love of all, Spirit, the Presence, the One or the God that adores me, whatever suits me at the time.

From experience I learned that somehow the Beloved knew what I needed even when I was such a mess I had no idea what end was up. When I was afraid, I got enough courage to walk through my fears in order to stand up for myself, to say no to what I didn't want and yes to what I did want, stepping out into my life in a new way. Did I have any idea what I was doing? Not at all! However, I quickly learned that this loving Presence was trustworthy, and that I would know what to do as I went along. Allowing myself to be guided, putting one foot in front of the other without any idea of what was around the corner, I just started.

Repeatedly, the Beloved's message came through loud and clear: *I was worth everything I ever wanted, and my life was meant to be happy.* It had nothing to do with how good I was or what I had accomplished—I was cherished simply because I existed. Period. And if this is true for me, it's true for you, too. There are no favorites with Divine Love—we are all the Beloved's precious ones.

What if, in every moment of the day, you were aware of a bubble of love around you, and within this bubble you *knew* that you were the most treasured person on the face of the earth? What if you had just messed up big time and within this bubble of love you were *still* life's most precious gift? If you absolutely, positively knew that this bubble of love was real one hundred percent of the time, how might your life change?

Good news! The bubble of love is real! The presence of Divine Love is right where you are, all around you and within you, cherishing you as its greatest gift. The Beloved's unconditional love is ever available to you, seeking your attention. If you're asking, "Why don't I feel this Presence?" one possibility is that the drama of human life is often so compelling that you think it's your reality, when all the while the love of a God that adores you is your true Reality.

You may have been emotionally beaten up by an idea of a judgmental God that may or may not love you depending upon how good you were, that may or may not answer your prayers and certainly wasn't where you would turn for comfort. If that's true for you I'm so sorry. That's someone else's view of God. It needn't be yours.

As you move through this book, please stay open to what's true for *you*. My experience belongs to me and your experience belongs to you. Our experiences may be very different because we are each beautifully unique. There's no right or wrong way to believe. *Remembering Who I Am* is about uncovering at a deeper level who you truly are—Life's precious gift, just as you are. Choose happiness. Choose you. You are worth it.

With love,
Jane

Chapter 1

I Am a Spiritual Being

A T THE MOMENT of divine creation we came into existence — specks of spiritual glow born from the greatest Light of all. Therefore, at our core we are all pure love, joy, peace, wisdom and every good thing we can imagine. It's who we are! I take a deep breath, breathing in the truth that I am a spiritual being, and within me I have everything I need to live a happy and fulfilled life. Even when I can't feel it, it's there. Even when I deny it, it's still there. No matter what horrible thing I think, say or do, my truth resides at the core of who I am. The beauty of Life itself is alive and well within me. It connects me with every other being, as we were created into existence from the same One. As spiritual beings we share the same spiritual DNA.

I Am a Spiritual Being

As a spiritual being I have a soul. My soul is the spark of light within me that's love, joy, peace, and wisdom — my divine inheritance. Peacefully and vibrantly alive in me, my soul guides me when I pay attention. It's like a trusted friend, one that knows my questions before I ever ask them, leading me to the answers I seek. Always available to me, it's my inner wisdom, my spiritual essence. When I don't know what to do, it's the part of me that does know. This comes in very handy in my daily life. In a challenging situation when a button has been pushed or I'm taking a comment personally I ask, "What aspect of my spiritual truth do I want to practice right now? Peace? Acceptance? Forgiveness?" Then I listen for the inner guidance that will take me to my destination of being peace, acceptance, or forgiveness in that particular circumstance.

With my willingness to pay attention to the wisdom of my soul I can change my thinking, my attitude and my behavior. It has nothing to do with the other person, as I'm the one who wants to have peace in my life. It takes practice! I celebrate my growth when I remember and am gentle with myself when I forget.

We are all part of the same One, born of the same Creator, our hearts beating to the same divine heartbeat. In my growing faith I can anticipate a shift in how I move through the world, a fresh awareness about everything and everyone around me.

Sometimes I can feel myself changing and sometimes I fall right back into my old ways. It helps me to remember to let myself off the hook when I goof and not to take myself so seriously. Will that comment that I took personally even matter a year from now? Do I really want to make a fuss (even in my own mind) about the small annoyances that catch me off guard? Are they worth my peace and happiness? Reminding me that I was born of the greatest Love of all, my inner guidance prompts me to remember the beauty of who I am.

～

*I am a spiritual being. Within me is everything
I need to be peaceful, happy and free.*

Awakening to My Truth

Who am I? What am I made of? Why am I here? The answers may not come easily when I try to answer them solely through logical reasoning. On its own, my mind can offer me solid guidance, but only based on what makes rational sense. There is beauty in supplementing the power of my mind with the wisdom of my soul. When I commune with the essence that flows through all of life, I'm listening to the One that created me. By doing so, I get a glimpse into the pure love that I came from and the absolute perfection that I am.

My soul, that part of me that is of God and is eternal, is forever whispering to me, reminding me of my magnificence. It invites me to remember that peace is my nature and that it is possible, in every situation, to become that peace. There is power in focusing on possibility, in looking for the good, in finding something to be grateful for, in trusting that life is on my side, to have a sense that I am okay and to let others know that they are okay, too.

Awakening to my truth is a process. In any circumstance I can choose love and I can be peace. I ask, "What would love do now? What would peace do now?" and then listen inwardly—I will know what to do.

~

*As I awaken to the truth, I am guided by
the love that is my true nature.*

The Divine Intelligence Within Me

I am part of a consciousness that is alive, intelligent and creative. In every moment of every day, I am guided by the wisdom of my soul, connecting me to the creative intelligence of the universe. Deep within me, it's who I am. Awakened to my spiritual nature, I'm reminded that I'm never alone, that my indwelling divine intelligence seeks my attention always.

At the moment of creation we were given free will, the mechanism through which we create our lives. We get to choose how we will respond to any situation, and the result of our choice is creative.

Are our responses mostly positive or negative? If they're mostly positive, we will create other positive experiences. If our responses are mostly negative, we'll attract more negative experiences. The good news is that once we realize that the intelligence of the universe is paying attention to our thinking, and if our life isn't what we want it to be we can start monitoring our responses and make adjustments.

Even when challenges appear, being aware that how we move through them is creative, we can change our attitude and move through it with optimism, faith, hope and gratitude. One conscious choice at a time, we can turn our life around.

As I awaken to my spiritual nature, I begin to differentiate between a message from my inner wisdom and a thought created in my mind. Messages from my inner wisdom are positive, encouraging and make me feel hopeful, even if I'm super-afraid about something, "You can do it! You have everything within you to move forward. I will show you how." Messages from my mind have a tendency to be negative. They are often wrapped around memories of the times I failed, "Give this some thought. It may not work. You don't have what it takes. Don't embarrass yourself."

When there's something I really want to do, I'm starting to have the courage to say yes to that inner guidance without letting the logical reasoning of my mind stop me. Even when my mind says, "That makes absolutely no sense; turn around and go the other way!" I step into my life in a new way, *owning* it, knowing that I'm worthy of the happiness life offers me.

That still, small voice of divine intelligence within me is always available. It's my spiritual cheerleader, an advocate, urging me forward, guiding each step. I can trust it. It's on my side. I can relax and follow its lead.

~

*In every moment of the day I'm guided by my own inner
wisdom. Knowing that it's trustworthy, I follow its lead.*

I Can Live a Balanced Life

It's not coincidental that the Earth is surrounded by a protective
atmosphere that encourages life—we would perish without it. It's
not by chance that plants offer a breathable atmosphere by adding
an abundance of oxygen and absorb carbon dioxide. It's not an
accident that the sea knows how to maintain a balance of salinity
and that the tides know when to come in and when to roll out, that
seasons know when to change, and that our bodies know how to
keep oxygen and temperature levels stable.

Life itself was generated by a perfect Creator, manifesting from
its own perfection. Of course plants and animals, the air and the sea
act in balance! They are in the flow of life, maintaining an existence
that is harmonious and abundant. The same is true for all of us!
We were created by the same Perfection, meant to flourish in a life
that's balanced, harmonious, abundant and free.

When I'm in the flow, I turn away from disharmony and
instead keep my attention on the perfection of the Creator within
me, through me, as me. Instead of being influenced by external
conditions, I stay balanced in the flow of life.

When my life is out of balance I'll know it—it doesn't feel good.
It's my reminder to take a deep breath, become centered, and seek
the guidance of my own inner wisdom. Sensing my next step, I
have the courage to take it, knowing that I am the only one who can
control the direction my life takes. Saying yes to a life of balance
and joy, I move forward in the sure knowing that I am creating the
life of my choice.

~

*I stay in the flow of the perfection within me, through
me, as me. My life is balanced, joyous and free!*

I Am Connected to Everything

Have you ever had a moment when you realized there was more to life than getting up each day, going about your business, and then doing it all again the next day? Somehow there's something bigger and greater going on? In one transformative moment we can have a sudden shift in consciousness that allows us to see the majesty of the life of which we are an integral part. As a glorious child of the Divine, we're each part of the interconnectedness of all life.

In all places . . . at all times . . . in all things . . . the presence of Love lives. It's the sun rising over the mountain tops and setting on the ocean's horizon. It's the eagle swooping down to catch its breakfast and the squirrel scurrying up the trunk of a nearby tree. It's the car engine that starts for our driving pleasure and the aroma of freshly brewed coffee. The realization that I'm connected to everything can happen at any moment. My view of life can be completely transformed as I delight in hugging a friend, becoming introduced to a new idea, or reading an inspiring book.

Either everything is God or it isn't. For me the God of my understanding is all things, at all times, in all situations. Love is real . . . alive . . . it is you and it is me. It's the neighbor next door, the empty lot on the corner and the cat down the street. It's the man mowing his lawn and the woman visiting a loved one in the hospital. On the surface we may look very different, but at our core we are connected by the Love that created us.

~

Stop for a moment, close your eyes, and imagine the feel of the sun on your face, bathing you with the warmth of its light. That same sun shines on all alike, no matter who they are or what their lives look like. The sun has no judgment about who is worthy of its warmth—instead it simply shines its light.

That same warmth directs seeds toward the soil's surface so that they might grow and flourish. It guides kelp toward the glint of sparkle on dancing waves, and it encourages flower buds to burst open in bloom. Just as the sun's rays shine equally on all who come out of the shadows to feel its warmth, we have within us a divine light that invites us to bask in the glow of its love and from that love, live our greatness.

We humans are a curious bunch—we often wonder what gift we can possibly bring to the world, not realizing that we already have within us everything we could possibly need to shine the light that we already are. We are each here to express our divinity in a way that is unique to us, as only we can do. Those transformative moments when we sense our connection to everything are also sacred reminders of our individual worth. We are each here on purpose. We matter in the world.

Today I'll take time to be fully present in every moment. When I forget the truth of who I am I'll turn my face toward the sun to remember that at any given time I can step out of the shadows of my life to feel its warmth, a reminder that I have within me my own light to shine.

$\sim$

As an integral part of all that is, I am connected with everyone and everything around me, created to shine the light that is me.

As a Spiritual Being I Am Immortal

What happens when I die? Will I truly live again?

Instead of fearing death, I become aware of the eternal cycle of life. Death of my earthly body is simply part of the perfection of life, for there is an essence within each of us that is the purest form of love and never dies. Rather, it only changes its form. My spiritual essence—the greatest part of me—is my soul. The human experience I'm having right now is part of the continuation of my soul's journey.

My soul guides me in each lifetime, like a trusted friend, one that knows my questions before I ever ask them, leading me to the answers I seek. As I open my heart and mind to this possibility, I can explore and embrace my own immortality, my soul's journey. If I can step back from what's happening in my physical world long enough to realize that my current human experience is just an infinitesimally tiny part of my eternal life, it helps to put everything in perspective.

As a lifelong atheist, if anyone would have told me that one day I would become a minister reflecting on immorality, I would have laughed! For the first 50 years of my life I never talked about God because why talk about something that doesn't exist? Then something happened.

On July 4, 1998, at a low point in my life, a tiny crack in my defensive armor appeared. Softly, gently, and with great purpose, in came the greatest Love of all. Suddenly I knew that first, the presence I was feeling was what people call God; second, I was profoundly loved and always had been; and, finally, it had simply been waiting for me to notice it. Today I know that if this is true for me, it's true for everyone . . . even on our worst days, when we have done and said things we regret, the Beloved thinks we're nothing short of magnificent! From that day forward everything changed.

Having no intellectual understanding of the Divine, my walk with the Beloved One has been purely experiential. For the next five years a personal, intimate relationship was fostered and nurtured. Staying awake—paying attention—my relationship with a God I knew as pure Love became the most important part of my life.

When I didn't know what to do, I learned that there was a part of me that did. It was as if the Beloved had given me the gift of knowing myself, "My cherished one, here is the gift of recognizing your own beauty, your own perfection. It is the part of you that is of me. You are me and I am you."

During that first five years, my faith grew and my life changed dramatically. I left my 30-year marriage without blame and without anger. I walked away from my 20-year career as an elementary school teacher and tried my hand in the business world, of which I knew nothing. All the while I was moving toward something that was calling me, though the "what" was elusive. With my focus on my God, I entered ministerial school, leaving some shaking their heads in bewilderment and at the same time commenting that, "You are the happiest person I know!" To this I would giggle quietly, whispering to myself, "Being in love with Love Itself does that to you."

~

Something shifted during the summer of 2003, and I yearned to be alone with the God that adored me in a way that was new. All I wanted was to worship. I would get up before dawn to jog, opening up a line of connection that would leave me almost breathless with its glory.

I was compelled that summer to begin losing weight, asking myself, *What's this about? I'm fine with how I look.* It seemed to have something to do with courage—you know how you have more confidence when you look your best? I began to ask, *Why do I need courage? What's up?* Without getting any answers, the weight came off easily. I was a picture of health!

That summer I began to understand why I needed to embrace a new level of courage . . . and faith. The stage was set for experiences I could never have imagined. I had gone to Asilomar, a retreat center in Pacific Grove, California, to our denomination's "summer camp," fully expecting a week of community and spiritual enrichment. However, the minute I stepped into my small room I knew that something holy was stirring. I stayed in my room all week, coming out only for meals. The rest of the time I sat in a straight-backed chair, poised with anticipation, and waited for "something."

That week I had three profound mystical experiences. In the

first two I was shown the true reality of Infinity, far past what we see and know on this earth plane. During the third experience my newfound awareness of immortality was born. I was shown a place I call The Womb. I saw it as a nesting spot in a safe, silent, round, dark space, like a womb. It was peaceful, housing tiny specks of light I knew were souls, that part of us that is of God and is eternal. Each was nestled into its own indentation, aware of others but with no need to interact. I was so filled with the purity and perfection of the Infinite One that I didn't want to leave.

These experiences were so huge, so deep, that they left me weeping, exhausted and a bit overwhelmed and frightened—hence, the need for courage. As always, the Beloved saw to it that I was provided with what was needed, holding me, wrapping its gentle energy around me as I processed the gifts I had been given.

I have continued to have ongoing revelation about immortality. Now I know that The Womb is one of many "nurturing places," states of consciousness where we go after each life experience. I have been to a few of them, and they are so real I could swear they were physical locations, though I know they are not. I suspect that souls can create whatever nurturing place best serves their transition from one life experience to the next.

~

Nurturing places serve two main purposes: First, it's where we process the life experience from which we just emerged. Second, there we get filled up with the love of the One that created us. It's where we remember who we are, and we bask in knowing that we are God's beloved one. Then we go on to express our divinity in another form because we are compelled to—that's why we exist.

Some people who have had near-death experiences actually experience a nurturing place, and it's so peaceful they don't want to return to their human body suit. I believe the place most call heaven is really a nurturing place and that there's more beauty even beyond that.

In the nurturing place a soul rests awhile, for a second or for a decade; it makes no difference. One soul may wait for another soul for some reason. We're all part of the same One, so we connect at many levels. In the appointed nurturing place, we may wait for the passing of another who will join us—a sacred agreement. It may be that the two souls, or more, will continue on into next lifetimes together.

A soul may choose to connect with another who is still living on this earth plane or another plane of existence. I was honored to be part of such an experience with the father of a friend, a man I never knew and who had been deceased for some time. While having dinner with my friend, she asked if I might be able to see her dad— she wondered if he was still in a nurturing place. I answered that I didn't know, that I had never had revelation about someone I had never met and who had already passed. Then within a few minutes I saw the soul of her father. He was silently communicating with me, as if he had expected my visit.

He appeared to be in a forested area, among the needles of a large redwood tree, nestled in very soft, light green mossy stuff that was tucked up close to the branch, in between the needles. It was almost as if the moss was part of the branch, held securely in place by the needles. There was no possibility of it being dislodged—he was in the safety of a nurturing place. He appeared as a very small, clear droplet, almost like a tiny drop of water, nestled into the soft green moss. There were other souls around him.

Every once in a while a breeze would move the branch just slightly, and I could feel the ebb and flow of the branch as it rocked in the breeze. It was as if God were cradling its cherished ones. I could feel this soul delight in being rocked! It was familiar to him; he anticipated and expected it.

Significantly, there was a very straight, thin gold line from my friend's dad to my friend. Way down in the right corner of the picture, as she moved, the line stayed straight and moved with her.

It was a direct connection. From this wise soul I knew:

✧ Wisdom was the first aspect of his own divinity that he remembered and embraced when he shed his human body. When my friend and her sister saw the doctors trying to resuscitate him, with his body flailing, he was already gone . . . what they did with his body didn't matter . . . he was already steeped in his own wisdom, the wisdom of the One who created him. What was awful for his family didn't matter to him—he was with Divine Love and all was well.

✧ I could feel his level of peace and joy and wisdom. He was steeped in it, a Sacred Wise One. He knew it, too. There was no conceit about it; he simply knew who he was.

✧ Sometimes he chuckled with the goodness of life! I could feel him delight in being alive.

✧ There was something about him that brought comfort to others. I believe he may have been a welcoming presence to those who were new to this particular nurturing place, although no words needed to be exchanged.

✧ The direct connection from her father's soul guides my friend today in many ways. Sometimes she gets a sense of his presence. His peace comforts her. He shares his joy with her so that her joy is multiplied.

In nurturing places we are nurtured because that's what God does. We soak it in because it's our nature to do so. We receive love, we give love. And we live, expressing the Love that is our true nature. We connect within and across lifetimes because we are all One, each a treasured piece of the tapestry of life that is created again and again.

The Beloved One forever knocks at the door of our consciousness, patiently waiting for us to recognize it. When we pay attention, we see that Life is all around us. We look outside our windows at the bare branches of trees that appear dead in winter. Within every branch creation is taking place; small buds are developing into leaves, curled into fetal-like positions, ready to unfurl when they feel the light of the sun on a warm spring day. They are alive in winter . . . vibrant . . . growing . . . we just can't see them.

It is much like us as we nestle into nurturing places.

We are born of God's love; it is who we are. It is our reality in every life experience and in the cycle of immortality. Instead of life and death, there is only change. Because we are immortal, our soul simply changes form and experiences again.

We take our consciousness with us, including the experiences gathered from each existence. There's no judgment about those experiences because to the Infinite One there is no right or wrong. In each incarnation, souls choose to have an experience of "something." It may be love, freedom, creativity, forgiveness or compassion, and it can show up in a myriad of ways. We incarnate onto the physical plane that brings us that experience.

There are souls that have chosen to incarnate as humans to live within a woman's womb just long enough to have an experience of that, and then they move on. We see it as miscarriage, when in reality the soul has experienced whatever it came to experience, and it's done. It returns to a nurturing place to process that life incarnation and to remember its own divinity, and then it creates again.

The only constant, on any plane of existence, is the love of a God that adores us. Everything else changes . . . it's supposed to.

～

Today I embrace my immortality. I listen to the
whisperings of my soul and my heart is at peace.

Dancing with Divine Love

The Beloved cherishes me. It wants nothing more than to dance with me, the one whom it has created. When I relax into its love I discover my own power, my own joy, with great expectation and purpose. I look around me at all the reminders to lovingly accept myself, just as I am. Flowers remind me that there's no competition with other flowers to see who is prettiest—instead they add to the beauty of life, each in their own way. The sun's rays don't compete to see who is shiniest—they just shine their light on everything that comes into contact with them. Wouldn't it be wonderful if we all knew it's safe to bloom and shine just as we are, each of us dancing our own unique dance with Divine Love?

I can take many avenues to get to my highest bliss—I choose all the time. Forever saying yes to my thoughts, feelings and beliefs, I am given the gift of free will from which to create my own life experiences, dancing with a universe that is alive, intelligent and accepts my choices as perfect, no matter what they are. Together we co-create my life.

When I start the dance and recognize it as such, I am compelled to keep it up because in it I feel special—beautiful, graceful, powerful, cherished. It begins when I recognize that I am not alone. The Beloved shows itself to me all the time. I sense it in my happiest moments, hear it in music, or see it in a loved one's smile. Then the dance begins in earnest, and my life is forever changed.

~

As my faith grows, I sense the Presence
and the dance with Divine Love begins.

Recognizing My Calling

I was created from pure potential—it's the core of who I am. Living my best life is my divine calling. Whether I believe it or not, I have the talents to reach my dreams, bringing my unique gift to the world. Up until this moment I may have overlooked my calling, and now the God of my understanding is nudging me toward my next step. It's time to lean into that voice of truth.

I begin by contemplating, "I am open to my calling," and then I pay attention. I sense the presence of my own inner wisdom. The first step will be revealed, often as my next positive thought. I'll take it, even if it doesn't make sense to me. Then I'll keep it up. I'll keep asking, listening, and then taking action. My faith muscle will grow strong as I have the courage to take one step at a time. That still, small voice within me is there as a pathway to the success of whatever it is I'm called to do. I choose to stay the course of its path. I can trust it. It's on my side. I gather my courage and follow its lead.

~

With gratitude, I stay the course of the path
that leads me to fulfilling my calling.

Chapter 2

I Am a Spiritual Being
Having a Human Experience

As a spiritual being I'll live forever, having many lifetime adventures in ways I can't even imagine. This time around I'm having a human experience with a lot of living to do! I have a hunch that my job here on earth, in this human body suit, is to learn to balance the perfection of my spiritual self with the ups and downs of my very imperfect human self.

Spiritually I really am perfect, made of the divine stuff of the Creator—peace, love, joy, wisdom, clarity and everything else wonderful. Humanly, I'm quick to judge others, I speak without considering the impact of my words, I eat the very food I said I'd avoid, I try to control everyone else's life because certainly I know what's best for them, and everything else that makes the human experience what it is. Being a spiritual being having a human experience is an interesting dance, one that takes a lifetime to explore.

Balancing My Spiritual Self with My Human Self

How do I balance my spiritual truth with my very human life? The Beloved tells me not to let my human insecurities shut down my spiritual greatness, that I'm a magnificent package, as is. I'm told that I've come to this time and space with gifts to give in a way that are unique to me alone. It may be the gift of my kindness to animals or my ability to listen to others. I may make the world a more beautiful place by painting a house, arranging flowers, or picking up litter during my daily walk. I might write a play, teach children, care for the elderly or become a volunteer. I'll know it's my gift because I'll enjoy doing it—time flies when I'm absorbed in it. My gifts may change, but one thing is sure, I'm supposed to share them. It's common for my human self to say, "You're not ready. You don't have enough education, money, practice, talent." If I keep letting my excuses get in the way my spiritual self—my inner wisdom—will remind me that I'm playing small.

I don't have to be perfect to give my gift. Mistakes, as well as successes, are part of the process. As a spiritual being having a human experience, I am already fully equipped to bring my gifts into realization, exactly as I am. When I listen to the wisdom of my soul and find the courage to follow its lead, I discover that I'm much more capable than I thought myself to be. I was created to let my dreams lead me to my greatest fulfillment.

When a brand new positive idea enters my mind, it's a God-thing, a connection between my spiritual self and my human self. The universe stands ready to co-create my good idea with me when I begin doing my part. As I take each step forward, the universe begins opening doors on my behalf. All of a sudden I'll get an unexpected invitation to participate in an event that's right in line with my dream, or there will be a phone call from someone in the same field, or a surprise check arrives in the mail that helps pave the way to my success!

Because we humans are full of our own opinions about life, I'm mindful of who I tell about my dream. The world is full of nay-sayers. I tell those who will be happy for me and stand ready to encourage me. I want only excited, happy energy surrounding me as I take every next step! If there's no one to tell, I can shout it out in the sanctuary of my own mind and heart. I can write about it in my journal, draw pictures about it or paste images about it to create a dream-collage. My determination and enthusiasm creates an energy that the universe will pick up, and I'm on my way!

Once I knew God was real my dream emerged. I wanted the whole world to know how Loved they are and they already have a relationship with the God of their understanding; they just may not have realized it yet. I wanted to find a way to open people up to the beauty of their own truth. This dream led me to become a minister, and spiritual seekers actually came to hear me speak about a God that adored them. What a joy! Then I started writing classes about building a personal relationship with the Divine. In facilitating those classes at my spiritual center, I watched the results emerge as participants realized that they had their own personal relationship with the God of their understanding. Their lives changed as their faith in their God and in themselves grew.

I happened onto Facebook almost by accident and a whole new avenue to living my dream exploded into being! Very quickly my Facebook page became a place where those on a spiritual journey came together as a huge spiritual family, with members from all over the world! Of course, this was no accident—it was the work of the Beloved, conspiring with the universe to open new doors from which my dream could emerge.

The next step came once I had been minister of my own spiritual center for seven years. After a short period of what I call divine discontent in which I suddenly felt confined in my role as minister of my church, I received a brand new thought that said, "It's time to retire in order to take your message out into the world." Without hesitation, I said yes and one month later I retired.

Retiring was only the beginning of the next step of living my dream! I started writing and I quickly found a publisher who was perfect for me. With the publication of my first book, *Choices: Choosing Me is OK,* I soon saw that my written word could reach a far greater audience than I could have ever imagined!

I wrote a three-part workbook series called, *How to Build a Relationship with the God of Your Understanding—Part 1: Start Where You Are, Part 2: Stepping into Change, and Part 3: Living Life Fully.* Many people have contacted me about their personal *Aha!* moments that came from answering the questions and doing the exercises in those workbooks! It's almost as if we'd been in a classroom together. Because the workbooks contain Facilitator Guides, they've been used for classes, retreats and book studies. 12-step sponsors are using them to work with their sponsees! My ability to write this series started way back when I taught elementary school and learned how to write curriculum. Nothing in life is ever lost. My dream continues. I'm speaking in churches and spiritual centers all over the United States and now internationally. My dream is coming to life because of my willingness to give my gifts, continually challenging the "I'm not good enough" stuff that rolls around in my head. The universe continues to open doors on my behalf. I'm not meant to play small, and neither are you.

What makes you so happy that time flies when you're doing it? It's either your gift or your gift may come out of it. Pay attention! You are meant to share it. The universe stands ready to open doors to help you share your gift. You do your part, the universe does its part—it's a glorious combination designed so that the world benefits from the gifts you share.

~

As a spiritual being having a human experience, I am willing to share the gifts I bring to the world.

Who Am I?

Who I am as spiritual beings is consistent—I am love, peace, joy. Who I am as a spiritual being having a human experience is fluid, depending on whether I'm tired or rested, at the dentist or with friends, on time or running late. I move through the day differently at work than I do at home, when I'm with strangers or with loved ones, listening to music or taking my car in for repairs.

The roles I play remind me that change is normal and natural, and within the circumstances of my life I change all the time. Occasionally I find myself restricted to seeing myself in a certain role—an unemployed person, a cancer patient, a busy manager, a parent or one who wishes they were a parent, a homeowner with costly repairs I can't afford or one who wishes they could own a home. I feel overwhelmed by the smallness of who I've become. It's time for me to remember that I'm more than the roles I play. I'm more than the circumstances of my life.

When I look up at constellations like the Big Dipper or Orion the Hunter, they seem a great deal like a big ladle or a hunter with his bow and arrow. The Big Dipper looks as if it could actually hold water. Orion appears to be taking aim, ready to shoot. But if I left earth and traveled closer to these pictures in the sky, I would soon see the pattern break up. Eventually the image would scatter and break down altogether.

Within any role I play in my human life, I can look closer to see that I'm much more than the roles I'm playing and the circumstances involved. Every challenging situation holds the promise of love because I am Love. When I'm angry, there is the promise of peace because I am Peace. Worrisome situations hold the promise of joy because I am Joy. Within every human experience is the opportunity to reach down into the beauty of who I am to find that which I seek. I will find it because it's there. It's who I am.

~

As I look past the roles I play, I find the
beauty and truth of who I am.

The Divine Teacher within Me

The very first aspect of God that I experienced—the one that awakened me—was Divine Peace. On a day when nothing felt peaceful (especially me!) there it was, a peace that defied explanation. It surrounded and filled me, and everything shifted. The circumstances of my life were exactly the same, but *I* was changed. If that kind of calm could be felt in an instant, and it was always available to me, why wouldn't I keep turning to it?

The problem was my mind, which was trained to believe God didn't exist. My brain asked me to doubt my inner guidance . . . to check to make sure it made sense . . . to get other peoples' opinions. My heart told me to just accept it . . . to know that Love would head me in the right direction . . . to believe that Life was trying to give me the kingdom. I chose the wisdom of my heart, and I sure am glad!

Today I follow divine direction. I often get a sense in my gut that my soul is waiting for my attention. I stop what I'm doing and silently ask, "What?" Then I listen with a depth that's deeper than my five senses—it moves me into the realm of receptive learner, waiting for directions from the Divine Teacher. I become aware of the connection and with eyes misty with gratitude, I sense the message. I become willing to follow.

~

Everywhere I go, in everything I do, I'm guided by the
Divine Teacher within me. I sense the
message and with faith, I follow.

Developing a Personal Relationship with the Divine

Sometimes God comes to me so softly I don't even notice that it's trying to get my attention. This may be true for you, as well. When was the last time you noticed the breeze running through your hair? Notice it—it's the Beloved reminding you that it's right where you are.

How many times have you turned on the radio in the car and a great song is playing, immediately causing a shift in your mood? Notice those times—it's the God of your understanding reminding you it's in your life always, tugging at the shirt sleeve of your consciousness, trying to get you to notice it.

It's easy to say, "That's not God; that's the wind, or that's the DJ deciding which music to play." Well, where and what do you think God is? It's everywhere, in everyone, and it's invested in your happiness and success.

Listen to the words of the next song you hear. Pay attention to the information in the next article you read or the story line of the next movie you watch. Notice the chance utterance of the next person you meet, or the whisper of running water, the scent of the flower in your neighbor's yard. All are avenues that Divine Love uses to get your attention. It's as if the Beloved is saying, "I speak to you all the time, inviting you to listen. I come to you in as many avenues as it takes for you to notice me so you'll know that wherever you are, I am."

Knowing God as Love is a powerful thing. It taught me that the world is good place, people are inherently good and life is on my side. I can trust that God is at center of everything, relax into each situation, let go of control, and know that I am safe.

Below are some ideas and activities that may move you toward building your own relationship with the God of your understanding.

- Start where you are. Can you think back to a time when you were able to believe that God/Life/the universe was on your side? Where things worked out for the best? Start there. Allow a feeling of gratitude to settle around that particular incident and bring it to mind when you think about your personal Higher Power.

- Set your intention for the day. Before you ever get out of bed . . . before you even think about what you need to do today . . . affirm something positive that will put a smile in your heart and maybe even on your face. Make it simple and personal to you. It can change from day to day, depending upon what's going on in your life. For example,

  - Today is a fine day and I do it well!
  - Today I smile for no reason . . . a lot!
  - Today I'll remember to pray . . . for any reason at all or just for the joy of it.
  - Today the only life I control is mine, and I'm worth my own time and attention.
  - When I'm unsure today, I'll remember that there's a part of me that knows what to do.
  - Today I'll like myself in every situation.
  - Today I look for ways to be kind to me.
  - Today I stay in Grace.
  - Today I'm safe. All is well.
  - Today is blessed. So am I.
  - Thank you, dear Life, for this day. I'm grateful!

Setting your intention encourages you to co-create your day with the God that you're building a relationship with. Even if you don't yet believe that it's true, act as if you do. It works!

- **Nurture yourself.** Your morning routine can actually be part of your spiritual practice. As you begin to move about, using the restroom, brushing your teeth and showering, stay in silence if at all possible. As you affirm that you will have a great day, allow your thoughts to stay positive.

- **If you're feeling tired.** On a day when you're feeling tired think to yourself, "What is it I need today?" Pretty soon something like this may pop into your head (if you let it), "I've had enough sleep. I'll move through this day well, knowing I'll sleep soundly tonight. Today I'll be cheerful with others and with myself." You'll find that your initial positive thoughts will flow into new ones, and you'll smile as you realize they're coming from the part of you that's always happy and at peace. You'll remember this positive interaction with yourself as your day progresses, and your optimism can actually change the course of your day!

- **When negative thoughts surface.** Your head may be filled with negative thoughts without you even being aware that they're there. If you begin to negate your new optimistic thoughts, know that your old habitual negativity is still at work. Bless those old thoughts as reminders of how you used to think, gently send them on their way, and give yourself credit for knowing the difference.

- **Give yourself gifts of self-care.** When you go to the closet to decide what to wear, let your heart guide you. Choose something that makes you feel beautiful, handsome, powerful, cheerful, wise, silly. . . whatever you're centered on for the day. Don't hesitate. Choose the outfit that catches your eye and smile as you congratulate yourself on a perfect choice! If you wear a particular uniform or suit because of work, buy yourself some fun underwear and wear that underneath! When you go shopping for a new toothbrush, don't just grab any toothbrush—buy one that's your favorite color, or has an unusual shape, something that's new and fun. Start noticing what you like about everything and choose that whenever possible.

- **Light a candle.** Light a candle or put a plant in the bathroom or your bedroom as you get ready for your day. Use soap that you enjoy as you bathe or shower. You're the guest of honor, and you're also the gift, so honor you!

- **Keep a notebook handy.** Notice the things you're doing that feel good. You have set your intention for the day. You've practiced nurturing yourself. Notice how your day changes and write it down. Make quick notes of the things that feel good, from enjoying your coffee to the smile you gave a coworker.

- **Create a Gratitude Journal.** Your gratitude journal will consist of three parts: 1. A gratitude list 2. Completing a sentence and 3. Writing a sentence.

- **Gratitude List.** At the end of the day, use your notebook to make a gratitude list in your Gratitude Journal. Choose five of your best day's events. For instance,

  - I'm grateful for my decision to have a good day.
  - I'm grateful that I said nothing instead of blurting out what I was really thinking.
  - I'm grateful that I got to the meeting on time.
  - I'm grateful for my pet's joyful greeting when I got home.
  - I'm grateful for laughing out loud at the TV show I watched tonight.

- **Completing a Sentence.** I'm proud of myself. After you've written your gratitude list, write this sentence and complete it: *I am proud of myself because . . .* For instance, I'm proud of myself because I was more aware of my thoughts, or I said nothing when I could have said something I'd regret, or I remembered to smile.

- **Writing a Sentence.** The last thing you'll write in your gratitude journal is the following sentence, or one like it that works for you: *Tonight I know I'm Loved.* Even if you're working at believing it, write it anyway (it's planting a new seed of thought in your mind). If possible, say it out loud.

- **Getting ready for sleep.** When you snuggle into bed know that the comfort of the God of your understanding is wrapping itself around you, loving you completely as you sleep. Say to yourself, "This has been a good day."

The Beloved constantly tugs at your conscious awareness. Let it in. Cultivate your relationship with this Presence that's awaiting your attention, just as you would cultivate a relationship with a new friend or lover.

$\sim$

Realizing how Loved I am is a grand journey. I notice the God of my understanding throughout my day.

Understanding My Ego

At every moment I'm choosing the kind of life I want to live. If I want to have a happy, optimistic life filled with abundance, I'll look for all things good—what's right in the world, what's right about my life personally, and what's right about me. As I look for the good in life, I'm making a conscious choice to see through God's eyes. If I find myself seeing negatively, I'm seeing through ego's eyes.

Science has discovered that ego is the part of our mind that's antiquated—it's been around since the cave man days when danger lurked at every corner. It taught us to beware of everything and everyone. Because food was scarce, we couldn't even trust those who were close to us for fear they would get what we needed. So we listened to the voice of our cautionary ego in order to stay safe. Today, that same ego-voice is still trying to protect us. It's not bad; it's just that it keeps us from growing. Ego's voice is loud "Look out!" while the voice of our inner wisdom is quiet and requires our full attention to hear it.

Today when I anticipate trying something new my ego-mind screams, "Be careful!" It uses many tactics to get my attention, reminding me that I'm not good enough and I don't have the right talent or education to get that job or try that new venture. In the past my ego yelled so loudly that I often didn't even try, not having any idea that the voice of my soul even existed.

Happily, today I realize that I no longer live in the cave-man days. I understand that part of my mind that's still trying to protect me with its very limited point of view. The good news is that because my ego is part of my mind, I can change it! On the spiritual plane, there is no competition. I don't have to be better than anyone else. My job is to be *me*, and to become willing to be the person *I'm* capable of being. It's safe to step out of my comfort zone, to reach past what's familiar. Whereas my ego wants me to be safe, my soul wants me to be free.

Turning toward the wisdom of my soul and away from ego becomes a natural awakening that happens with experience. After I've "banked" a few experiences of trusting my inner wisdom, I can fall back on those examples the next time I hear my ego trying to stop me. The cave man days are gone. Today I choose to look through the Divine eyes of possibility and say yes to the life that's waiting for me.

~

I turn toward love, instead of fear; and wisdom, instead of worry. Today I choose freedom!

In the Darkness I Am Safe

In very difficult situations I might ask, "Where is God? Why does God allow this to happen?"

I forget that when the Creator created everything-that-is, it did so with great confidence, giving us all the free will to explore each life experience without judgment. We aren't judged when our life looks messy or when we're celebrating our successes. To the question, "Where is God in this?" the answer is that Spirit is at the center of it, as pure love. Under all the mess and the fear and the negativity, Divine Love is alive and shining. If I choose to look for Love, my life will change. It's possible to shine the light of my own inner wisdom on every challenge, learning to embrace myself by growing in acceptance, forgiveness, and compassion.

My constant guide, my soul, is my place of calm within the storm. As my light in the darkness, it sees the big picture of my life when I'm whirling in the midst of the moment's confusion. Turning toward the light opens me up to the faith and courage in which I grow through difficult times instead of feel defeated by them. Stepping into the illuminating wisdom of my soul helps me to accept what is, face my angst, and then embrace the truth and healing wisdom my angst offers.

~

There is power in allowing my inner wisdom to shine its
light in the darkness of my very human life.

The Strength of My Character

Climbing out of the hole of victimization really does build character. Consciously facing my circumstances helps me realize that there's a lot more to me than I ever imagined! Somewhere from deep within I find strength and wisdom that before had been off my radar screen.

Now I see it! I not only see it, I pull from it and discover that there's a whole well-spring of good within me that I never knew existed. The process isn't one bit easy, but without it I don't learn of the stuff from which I'm made.

My perspectives and priorities are born from my experiences. I won't recognize my full worth unless I've been mired in feelings of unworthiness and dug my way out of it. It's part of what connects me to the human race.

We've all done things we wish we hadn't. We've all had loss. We've all been afraid. We all want to be loved. Every struggle becomes a divine stepping stone, bringing us to who we are today. We've learned to be a lot gentler with ourselves and with others. I can offer a hand to those still mired in victimization. If they're ready they'll grab hold, and if not I can keep them in my prayers while they build a bit more character. Somehow, I understand the chaos that they may be feeling. We're all much more alike than we are different, and in our own way we'll build the strength of our character.

～

Falling down and pulling myself back up strengthens me.
As I consciously face every life circumstance,
I build the strength of my character.

Becoming the Watcher

There came a time when I became the watcher of my dance between fear and courage. Fear lurked in the back of my mind, ready to jump out at a moment's notice. Courage made its home my heart space, quietly present in all situations. Much of my fear came from old beliefs, many adopted from childhood—wasn't everyone afraid of not having enough or being good enough? My courage came from the unlimited possibilities born of my newfound faith—I *already* had enough, I was *already* good enough. I started to discern where each feeling was located and how it showed up. I noticed what thoughts held me back and what fear's "It won't work" felt like in my gut. I noticed the excited butterflies in my stomach when I thought about moving forward, which was often how courage got my attention. I got to know and understand how fear and courage showed up in each situation.

Once courage started leading the way, the old restricting fear-beliefs came up again and again to try to stop me, trying to make me turn around and go back. At the same time, the quiet voice of my soul . . . my inner cheerleader . . . urged me to keep moving forward. Today, as I learn more and more about myself, I remain the watcher, knowing that fear and courage are both parts of *me*. It's my life, and I am the one who makes a conscious decision about which aspect of myself I'll listen to.

~

Fear and faith are both aspects of me. In understanding them, I make a conscious decision about what to do in any situation.

Owning My Fears

Fear has often stopped me from taking that next step toward being joyously fulfilled. I let it prevent me from saying what I needed, standing up for myself, or telling someone no. Fear can keep us from asking the boss for a raise, taking a class, beginning our own business, or introducing ourselves to a potential new friend. Fear often keeps us tucked tightly into a very small box—our comfort zone.

Owning my fears, with the intention of consciously learning from them and then moving through them, has been empowering, like getting to know and understand the bully who picks on you. Before I knew God was real my fear-bully was my identification with victimization. Seeing myself as a victim eventually led me to learn from some of the scariest times in my life. I never intended to end up in a 12-step program, and yet my time in recovery was probably the most important period of my life. I never intended to get a divorce, and yet today I'm grateful for every moment of my marriage and then for releasing it without blame or anger. I never intended to leave the security of my teaching career, but without it I wouldn't have become a minister, speaker and writer. I ended up growing strong by moving through my fears!

When I listen to the whisperings of my own inner wisdom, fear becomes a reminder that I'm at the edge of my comfort zone and that transformation is at hand. It's the journey from where I am to where I want to be on the other side.

When there's excitement mixed in with the worry, it's an indication that the journey is mine to take. Life is offering me the kingdom if I am willing to accept it.

I let the Beloved hold me in my fear until I finally feel the presence of my own inner strength. I remember that I don't have to figure out how to do it because I'll be guided as I move forward. The God of my understanding takes care of the journey *and* the outcome—I all I need to do is my part. I remember all the times when I've been courageous, and I know I can do it again. I'm becoming a willing and grateful student as I learn from every aspect of my life.

～

I'm willing to learn from my fears.
Growing through them strengthens me.

The Stories I Tell Myself

I'm really good at making up stories about what happened in my past, trying to make sense of it all. Those stories become my memories. As I've become more aware of who and what I truly am, my memories have softened. What were once demoralizing situations that left me feeling embarrassed, ashamed, resentful and angry have morphed into opportunities that helped me stretch, change and grow. From them I learned self-understanding, self-compassion, and self-forgiveness. I realize today that such situations connect all of us—they're part of the human condition. It's now easier to offer understanding, compassion and forgiveness to others. What once felt so personal is in reality common to many. The situations may be different, but the feelings are the much the same.

I've given my most painful memories to the Beloved for safekeeping—if I need to visit them I can. I visit them less and less these days. Today I often choose selective memory. I remember the things that put a smile on my face. I remember the difficult times only to reflect on what I learned and how I grew stronger because I walked through them. Today I choose to think about what's right in the world, and that includes my memories.

~

I tell a new story about my memories, one that's uplifting, optimistic and filled with compassion.

I'm an Energy Magnet

Have you ever noticed that unhappy people seem to attract situations that cause them even more unhappiness? Then there are the happy people who appear to have all the luck? It's not coincidental. There's a reason it shows up like that. Science has now proven that everything is energy, including us. The universe is magnetic; therefore, everything has a magnetic frequency.

Our thoughts, and the feelings that propel them, have magnetic frequencies, either landing us on a positive frequency or a negative frequency. There's no judgement about it—the universe is simply responding to what's alive in us. Our thoughts and feelings act like a magnet, attracting the people and situations that share the same frequency.

For me this is helpful. If I keep finding myself in less-than-satisfying circumstances, I can take a look at what's been rolling around in my head—mostly positive thoughts or negative? Gratitude or complaining? Acceptance or judgment? A focus on peace or stress? I often find that the biggest culprit is what I'm saying about myself—that's where a lot of that complaining, judgment and stress resides!

Then I remember that at the moment of creation we were given the free will to choose our perspective, our attitudes and our behavior. Where we put our focus magnifies our magnetic frequency. My thoughts and feelings create my attitudes and behaviors. I can choose to see a challenging circumstance as an opportunity to grow or not.

My favorite Al-Anon quote fits here: *I don't have to like the situation, but it is imperative that I like myself in it.* Liking myself helps me pay attention to my choices. It helps keep me on the "good-feeling" frequency, which attracts to me other people and circumstances that are on that same frequency.

You can bet that when I somehow get out of sync with that good-feeling frequency, it feels yucky enough to remind me to make some quick attitude adjustments to get myself back on track.

Today my life is incredibly blessed—I am filled with gratitude for the people and situations that surround me! Not everything is glorious, but when I use the challenges as an opportunity to like myself, I can feel the change in my energetic frequency. I know that right in the middle of the situation my positive outlook is raising my magnetic frequency, creating a space for wonderful outcomes to occur.

～

I am an energy magnet, and today I attract positive people and situations into my life.

My Mom Died

As a spiritual being I know that I'm immortal, that I will live and have experiences in many different lifetimes. As a human being in the middle of this particular life experience, I do my best to be fully present in the moment, no matter what that moment looks like.

This year, 2015, my Mom died. She was 98 and ready to go. In fact, she was determined to die. It wasn't that life was horrible; it was just that she was done. "What's the point of living any longer? I'm ready to go now." Who was I to argue? She knew what she wanted.

I've always had a special relationship with Mom, so when she moved into an assisted living facility close to my home I spent every afternoon of the last five years of her life with her. It was my choice. I had a huge wish to make the end of her life as smooth and happy as possible. We planted flowers in pots on her balcony, worked jigsaw puzzles and took a daily walk in the halls of her building. I watched her abilities slowly decline and was uplifted by her determination to do the best she could with what she had. By example, she taught me how to grow old with dignity.

At the beginning of her 98th year Mom told the whole family that she wanted to die. Bless her heart! Her declaration made her dying okay for herself and for everyone else. As an atheist she told me, "When you're done, you're done." She was unafraid of being "done."

As a minister and one who experiences a glorious relationship with the God of my understanding, it was interesting to be in this process with Mom. We never talked about God or any kind of a Higher Power because she didn't believe that anything like that existed. That was okay by me! I respected my mom enough not to try to push my beliefs on her. After being an atheist for the first fifty years of my life, it's not hard for me to hang out with non-believers.

Instead of talking about spiritual things, we got down to particulars. Mom talked about her death a lot. She wanted it to be fast and pain free. She wanted me to be with her. She had a file ready with everything that needed to be done after her death: who to notify, arrangements to be made, and her memorial was planned down to the last detail. Her memorial was her last great hurrah and because I would be the officiant, she felt comfortable knowing that her wishes would be followed.

As Mom talked openly and freely about her death I listened closely to what *she* wanted and didn't try to pull my wishes into it. I didn't say, "Oh, don't talk like that; you'll live to be 100!" like others had exclaimed. Mom didn't want to live to be 100. Because I had been with her so much it was easier to accept the idea of her dying.

One month after Mom's 98th birthday she got her wish. Standing at the bathroom sink she had a heart attack. I met the ambulance at the hospital. Knowing that she had a DNR (do not resuscitate order), the doctors quickly confirmed with me that this was the end. Quietly in my mind I thanked the Beloved for this gift. After telling Mom what the doctor said, I added, "This is what you have wanted. It's your opportunity to start the dying process," to which she replied, "Good! Let's do it!" She was actually excited! She was quickly loaded up with pain medication and hospice was called. As each development unfolded, my prayer was one of surrender, "I give her to you, dear Beloved One, because you know the big picture for what's happening in this moment." By evening we were back in her room at the assisted living facility. My beautiful, atheist Mom was truly being held in the arms of Grace.

I stayed with Mom for the next four days, at the end of which she passed. I was grateful to know exactly what she wanted so that I could speak for her when she couldn't speak for herself. The first two days she was medicated but lucid, and family came to say their goodbyes. She had given me strict instructions about those goodbye visits, as she didn't want long, drawn out conversations filled with teary emotion. So before each small group had their visit, I spelled it out for them and then hovered by the doorway, watching to make sure Mom was okay. During two of the visits someone said, "You'll see Papa (my dad) on the other side." This almost made me chuckle because I knew Mom didn't believe it. At the end of the day I said, "Hey Mom, what did you think when you heard people say you'd see Dad on the other side?" She answered, "I don't believe a word of it! I just let them say it because it made them feel better." We laughed! There we were in the course of her dying, and we were laughing! The Beloved's work, no doubt . . .

The last two days Mom was deep in the process of leaving her body, and finally, in the middle of the night, she was almost there. We had likened her death to nearing the finish line. At the end, as I held her close, I encouraged her, "You're almost there. You can do it. Cross the finish line." I think it was the greatest gift I ever gave her, and therefore the Beloved's greatest gift to me. She passed as I held her, while the greatest Love of all held us both. Mom may not have believed in God, but it was abundantly clear that the Beloved believed in her.

The next morning I realized that the most glorious thing had happened! Mom's spirit was alive in me! I could feel her presence easily—she was a shiny speck within my heart. My heart space was her nurturing place, where she could rest awhile until she was ready for her next life experience. Instead of mother and daughter, this began a new relationship as spiritual beings.

The following morning when I awakened, Mom was gone from my heart space. Instead I could sense her presence in the vastness of the universe. It was glorious! She was part of all that is . . . in all places . . . at all times. She was home. My heart is filled with joy as I write this! I have no need to hold on, as I want her to fly and be free to be whatever she wants to be. She lives. The same is true for all of us. We will lay down our human body suit to live again and again and again.

When the One created us as spiritual beings, made from the same stuff as the Creator, immortality was included. We will never die. We have forever to live in the glory of Life itself. It's a reminder for me not to take this life experience too seriously . . . not to take myself too seriously . . . to have fun and be silly . . . to love others and love myself. God is indeed very, very good.

~

As I let go of the ones I love, I release them into the
glory of Life itself, where they are held by
the greatest Love of all.

Unexpected Blessings

Through my life challenges I've grown to understand that there's a greater purpose for my life than just getting through each day. There was a reason for everything. All those struggles created a pathway to the emergence of who I am today. As I grew through each difficulty, sometimes kicking and screaming, I became stronger and wiser, more filled with faith in the God of my understanding and more filled with trust in myself. I'm aware that within what looked like horrible circumstances lay unexpected blessings. I didn't see them then, but now I realize how much I grew through each struggle.

I have wondered, "Why am I here? What is my purpose?" Sometimes the question has been answered after one of those periods of huge crisis. I ask, "What caused that? Why me?" I've come to understand that I have a greater purpose, one I never could have anticipated. I take that challenging experience, with all its myriad feelings and memories, and build on what I learned from it. Why did I survive? What did I learn about myself, my relationship with the Beloved, my relationships with others, and my relationship with life itself? Suddenly I become open to a new direction for my life. I may not know what it is, but something within me knows. As I pay attention to my own inner wisdom I realize that an unexpected blessing was born out of crisis—an awareness of courage, wisdom, tenacity, endurance, and the power of my own strong will that was there all along. Now that I realize that I'm much more capable than I thought myself to be, I'm filled with energy and renewed purpose. I have grown into my next step, whatever it may be, and I'm ready to live it!

*Within each life challenge hides a blessing as I realize
I am much more than I thought myself to be.*

Chapter 3

I Am Awakening

MANY GO THROUGH LIFE having no idea that they are a spiritual being. They think that life happens to them, so they enjoy the good moments and brace themselves for the bad ones. Without the realization that they are part of the divine flow of Life itself, they don't realize that Life is responding to them—to their thoughts, beliefs, and actions. They don't know that they have within them everything they need to live a life of freedom and fulfillment. They don't know that they are Love in form.

Awakening to the truth is a huge God-thing! All of a sudden there's *choice!* In every minute they can consciously choose how to respond to whatever is going on in their life. They can choose to believe that they are cherished by a God that adores them, just as they are. They can choose to follow their own inner wisdom. Awakening is simply waking up to the truth, and it changes everything!

One of the reasons I wrote this book was to create a safe space whereby readers like you might move into a personal awakening to the truth and the glory of who you are. You come alive with the richness that Life has to offer, knowing that you are worthy of every happiness, simply because you exist. You don't have to do anything to earn the prize—you *are* the prize! Life stands ready to give you the kingdom if you are ready to accept it.

If you've been on a spiritual path for some time and have already had a spiritual awakening, my prayer is that you'll use this book to deepen that awareness, trusting that it's safe to travel down new paths that you may have never even known existed. With a spiritual awakening comes a deeper faith and trust in your God, yourself, and your life. Together, let's explore the options.

Why Am I Here?

Inevitably, those of us on a path of spiritual awakening ask questions like: Who am I? Why am I here? What is the purpose of life? What is the purpose of *my* life?

During our days we wear many hats and engage in countless roles: we are children, parents, lovers, friends, talkers, thinkers, meat-eaters, vegetarians, employers, employees, dog-lovers, cat-lovers, the person who empties the trash or the person who reminds the other that it's time to take the trash out. In each given role we are offered a plethora of emotional choices: we are strong or weak, confident or unsure, peaceful or anxious, accepting or judgmental, motivated or procrastinating.

All are opportunities to interact in our very human environment. At the same time, past our roles, gender, socio-economic status, race, or age, lays a hidden wholeness within us . . . our spiritual essence . . . that shines a light on all that we do. The truth is that we are a glorious blend of human experience and spiritual perfection.

Who I believe I am will set the course of my life, determining how I will live. If I'm unsure of who I am I'll live tentatively, guessing at what I should do next, often trying to be what someone else wants me to be. But when I feel comfortable with myself I live courageously, taking responsibility for all of my life, always moving in a direction that feels right for me even if others are asking me to go a different way.

Being on the path of spiritual awakening is about saying yes to life, just as it is, learning from it, growing through each experience. It's knowing that I'm never alone, that the light that shines within me *is* me. The purpose of my life is to be joyously happy and fulfilled. I am the only one who can make the choices that lead to my highest happiness and fulfillment. When I listen to my innermost wisdom, it will shine a light on each next step, guiding me in the right direction.

~

The purpose of my life is to be joyously happy and
fulfilled. I say yes to my purpose, beginning right now!

Leap of Faith

Some leaps of faith are huge, and others are smaller. When I first discovered that God was real, I practiced going from faith in myself, which was pretty shaky at the time, to faith in something that I couldn't even see but could *feel*. Getting to know the God of my understanding was a one-step-at-a-time adventure!

I tested the waters of faith by experimenting with the Beloved to see what would happen. One time when I was going to set a boundary I took a chance, "I'm turning this over to you. Tell me what to say and how to say it. Help me be gracious with the person's reaction, no matter what it is." The whole situation was amazing! I could actually feel the presence of Love as I stood in front of the other person! Even though my stomach was doing nervous flip-flops, my words flowed and my demeanor was peaceful. I had no need to hang onto the outcome. That leap of faith led to another as I prepared to make a difficult phone call. Instead of worrying about it and trying to control the situation, I once again prayed to be guided and let go of expectations. And once again it worked!

With each instance, my faith in myself was returning as I discovered an inner wisdom that I could trust. After many such experiments, I came to the conclusion that God is worthy of a leap of faith, and so am I.

~

With every leap of faith—big or small—my trust in my own inner wisdom grows.

Leaning into Love

I'm aware of the many facets of human love—the love we have for our spouses, partners, children, family, friends, pets and even strangers, and the ways in which we feel love from them. Human love connects us with others in ways that remind us that we're part of a greater whole. When I can stand with someone who is experiencing loss of any kind and simply be there for them while they navigate the feelings that go along with it, my caring becomes part of their experience. When I have felt betrayed by another and I can get to a place of forgiveness, my life is uplifted. When I've hurt another and offer my sincere apology, I feel the grace of thankfulness. When I can put another before myself (which often includes pets) I know the sweetness of selflessness. The love we humans have for each other shows up in many ways, reminding us that we all want to love and be loved in return.

We are more than the love we experience humanly. Divine Love is alive and well within all of us, including our families, friends, pets and strangers. Today I remember that Divine Love is the light that shines bright within me, no matter what horrible thing I've just thought, said or done. It is the Love that comforts me when I'm grieving, the Love that gives me courage when I'm afraid, the Love that guides my next steps when I'm filled with doubt, the Love that helps me like myself when I look in the mirror. With a Love that is unquestionably accepting, I'm invited to remember that everything I have done in my life has brought me to where I am now, and who I am in this moment is perfect. Who wouldn't want to lean into such a Love as that?

Once I realize how Loved I am, everything else takes care of itself. A by-product of living daily immersed in the love of a God that adores me is that giving and receiving love in my daily life becomes lots easier. I show up more authentically, as I have nothing to hide. I trust the path my life is taking because I have learned that Divine Love is trustworthy. I can let go of the need to control the lives of those I love—instead I surrender them to the greatest Love of all. Embracing the Love that is my truth helps me share human love with those around me.

～

*Leaning into the greatest Love of all helps me fully
embrace the human love in my life.*

Gratitude as a Bridge

Gratitude is perhaps the single most important relationship I can foster with the universe. It's the bridge between where I am now and where I want to be. In the middle of a mess, looking for something to be grateful for automatically uplifts me. It's impossible to be in the mode of, "I hate this. I don't deserve it. What's going to happen to me?" and gratitude at the same time. Gratitude shifts my perspective from being mired in negativity to searching for the positive, "I'm still breathing. God is here. I'm not alone. This too shall pass."

Every day offers an opportunity to look for gratitude as I face unexpected interruptions, delays, and unwanted surprises. When I'm feeling overwhelmed by the situation it's hard to move through it with grace, which is my goal. Looking for something to be grateful for is like a drowning person swimming toward the surface of the water. The way has been shown! I come up with one gratitude, and then another. The universe senses the change in me, and a vast array of possibilities start to move into action. The person who has loosened access to those solutions is the one who has changed their perspective, and it's me! My shift in consciousness has activated the loving, creative, intelligent universe on my behalf.

Gratitude is an ongoing prayer, connecting me with the highest part of myself. It puts me in touch with my own inner wisdom, that part of me that's never been hurt, disappointed or afraid. It allows me to sense my courage, resilience and strength. Gratitude is the bridge back to my truth and to the life I choose for myself.

～

With every reason I find to be grateful, I access my own inner strength and ignite a loving universe into action on my behalf!

Are My Beliefs Really True?

Because I know that my thoughts are creative, every once in a while I find myself exploring a thought in my mind and wondering, "Where did that thought come from? Do I really believe it? How long have I been carrying it around in my head, acting as if it were true?" It's then that I realize it's time to investigate the belief behind the thought.

Beliefs are repeated thoughts that have strong feelings attached to them. Some people believe that a daily teaspoon of honey promotes good health, and that belief is true for them. Others believe that honey will actually do harm, and that belief will be true for them. Some believe that by nature, life is hard. Because they expect life to be hard, they will attract to them people and situations that prove that indeed, life is hard. Others believe that the universe is a friendly place and by staying open to the good it has to offer, good will come their way. Even in challenges they expect good to show up, which it usually does. Some try hard to stay off of all western medicines, believing that there's a better way to take care of their body. As they practice alternative health care, many are healed in the process. My mom believed that her numerous prescriptions are what kept her alive and well, and her belief stood her in good stead as she lived 98 healthy years. What we believe generally becomes true for us.

Many grew up buying into beliefs about money because that's what their family believed. Comments were overheard from adults: There's not enough money to go around, you have to work hard to get money, money is evil, rich people are greedy. As I began investigating my beliefs about money and prosperity, I realized how many of those familial beliefs I had simply adopted as my own. It gave me the opportunity to take a fresh look at what I believe is possible today and dump those old beliefs—what a relief! As I let go of the old and embraced the truth that we live in an abundance universe and God's will for me is complete happiness, prosperity started making its way into my life in the form of unexpected income, exciting opportunities, and creative new ideas.

Beliefs will be true for the believer, and their lives will reflect that belief. How much do I believe I deserve? What I believe I deserve either sets me up for limitation or becomes an avenue to abundance in every area of my life.

If one area of your life isn't working as well as you'd like, explore your beliefs about it. Is your belief limiting you or setting you up for success? You were meant to be gloriously happy! As a spiritual being having a human experience, there is a part of you that knows the unlimited possibilities for happiness—all you need to do is chose them. Take the time to listen to the part of you that forever guides you toward health, wealth, joy and fulfillment. Replacing even one old belief will change your life. Don't take my word for it—try it!

~

I let go of beliefs that are no longer in my best interests and adopt new beliefs that bring me the happiness I deserve.

Divine Discontent

With a spiritual awakening comes the call to action. No longer am I willing to settle for life as it has been. Change takes place all the time, and I'm changing, too. What was once a dream come true may now be something I need to leave behind in order to keep evolving into the person I want to be.

Sometimes I've been in a job, relationship or a pattern of behavior that used to bring me pleasure but is no longer satisfying. Nothing has changed except me—I'm bored, antsy and envious of others. It feels really crummy but it's actually good! It's called divine discontent. It often comes right before a big shift or next step–it's the God of my understanding nudging me forward.

Divine discontent happens when something new beckons and I'm hesitating. I'm trying to find satisfaction in a situation that's become too small for me. I try to stay there because it was once what I wanted. I feel like I'm questioning myself, "I got what I wanted and now it's not good enough? What's up with that?" Yet it no longer brings me happiness, thus the discontent.

When I'm in divine discontent I ask, "Am I trying to settle for a life that now feels cramped? If so, what's stopping me from moving out of the status quo and into whatever's calling me? Fear? Procrastination? Habit?" Listening to the gentle encouragement of my soul, I trust that I'm okay, and then I take tiny steps forward.

I practice saying yes to my new life instead of no. Knowing that I'm not too old, too unhealthy, too broke or too wounded to start, I don't settle for anything less than what I deserve.

~

Paying attention to divine discontent, I open to a greater reality and step out into the life that is waiting for me.

The Willingness to Let Go

The more my faith grows, the greater my willingness to let go of anything that may get in the way of the life I'm meant to live. I'm grateful for the ability to let go of who I thought I was supposed to be. Before I knew God was real, I would have described myself as a dedicated mom, grandma and school teacher who would live my life vicariously through my grandchildren after retiring from the classroom, knitting baby blankets for each new arrival.

Whereas that's a wonderful path for many active and loving grandparents, it's no longer my dream. Now I can't even imagine living my life through anyone or anything except the Beloved. I'm creative in ways that are new and exciting—writing books and articles that are read by thousands and creating classes that are taught in New Thought centers across the country and even outside the United States. I travel and speak at different spiritual centers and events, putting me into community with people who are on a spiritual path, just like me. It feels deliciously exciting and rewarding. I gave away those knitting needles long ago!

Letting go can show up in lots of areas of our human lives. There is great power in letting go of drama. Usually drama is created because someone is acting in a way that I don't agree with. It's easy to be righteous and judgmental, creating stories in my head, but my own negativity doesn't feel very good. Letting go means allowing everyone to be on their own path, accepting them as they are. It makes life so much easier! Whereas I used to think that drama kept life interesting and gave me something to talk about, now I find it tiring and time consuming. Letting go frees me up to live the best life *I* can live, creating a space in my mind for new ideas to emerge instead of the entanglements of judgment. In the process, I like myself!

In awakening to the truth of my own unlimited possibilities, I'm much better at letting go of self-imposed limitations. Done (most of the time) are the thoughts of "I'm not good enough." Instead I let myself be guided by the Beloved One. Because my God is trustworthy, I have found a courage I never knew I had—the courage to say yes to a glorious life that the Universe lays at my feet, if only I will receive it. Today I say yes! No longer does my fear stop me because the new me is courageous! I'm still scared, but I no longer let it stop me. That's courage!

I invite you to take some time to gratefully consider all the places where you've already let go. If you've let go of a relationship that was no longer in your best interest, that's it! If you've let go of guilt because you realized you were doing the best you knew how at the time, good for you! If you've let go of blame and embraced forgiveness, your reward is freedom! I bet you can find a lot about yourself and your life that you can appreciate.

There is much about letting go for which we can be grateful. It often begins with letting go of the old so that the beauty of who you are—and the life you were meant to live—can emerge. Go for it!

～

With gratitude, I'm willing to let go of anything that keeps me from living my happiest life.

Just One Step

It does me no good to compare myself to others I admire as they do the things I want to do. I always fall short. My shoulders slump and my eyes look down in automatic dejection. My stomach does fear-filled flip flops with the idea of me even trying to compete! My memory brings up all the times that I didn't follow through or I tried and failed. My ego reminds me that I'm much better off doing what I'm doing instead of venturing into the unknown where it's dangerous because of all those who are better equipped to do what I'm considering. That's when the glow of my inner light—my personal cheerleader—shines bright enough to catch my attention. Out of my dejected stupor, I lean in to listen.

Paying attention to my cheerleader's divine guidance, I feel the glow of the limitless possibilities that not only exist in the world— they exist in me. Each possibility begins with a single thought, an idea that's ready to be birthed with one lone next step. It may be the idea to plant a garden, help an elderly neighbor with their recycling, or become a community volunteer. When I turn away from the negativity that's trying to stop me and say yes to that inner nudge, a seed of faith is planted in the soil of my most positive thoughts. I don't need to know *why* I'm taking the next step or where it's leading—it *feels* right and generates a sense of excitement, so I do it!

When I'm in the flow I thrive, even though I have no idea what I'm doing or what the outcome will be. My personal cheerleader nudges me forward with every next step, reminding me that I'm not alone, that I'll always be guided and that I matter in the world.

Just as if I were planting a garden, I feel the profound satisfaction that comes from my connection with the earth as I tend the soil that feeds the seed that I planted. The seed of self-esteem begins to grow and blossom. When I help the elderly neighbor with her recycling I begin a friendship that reaches deep into a feeling of loneliness and separation from the world that I didn't even know was there.

I wonder, who has been given the greatest gift here? Volunteering on a regular basis connects me with others in activities far more rewarding than I could ever imagine, a reminder that we all matter.

I was meant to bring the gift of who I am to the world. Comparison with others is self-defeating because it's out of alignment with recognizing *my* gifts, *my* beauty, *my* way of showing up. When I'm in the flow of divine guidance I say yes to each next step that's in front of me, doing it *my* way. It will lead to another next step, and then another. Just like the soil feeds the seed in the darkness where we can't see it, behind the scenes the universe works on my behalf to manifest a life that's richly fulfilling. Together, the seed and the soil bring about the beauty of the plant. Together, the universe and the seed of my authentic self brings about the beauty of who I am, just as I am.

Today I trust the changes Life asks me to take. Even if the next step seems scary because it's new, I ask myself if I'm willing to believe that I'm good enough, smart enough, worthy enough, and loveable enough take it. After all, if the Beloved planted the thought in my head, don't I think the Beloved believes that I'm good enough, smart enough, worthy enough, and loveable enough to do it? Today I say yes to every positive, enriching next step.

～

*Paying attention to my inner cheerleader, I take each step
forward in bringing the gift of ME to the world.*

Listening to the Secret

Paying attention to divine direction is like hunkering down within myself to listen to the most important secret in the world. Something within me tells me that the secret is a gift that will change my life, so accessing it becomes a priority. In order to hear it, I must be quiet and attentive, creating an atmosphere of receptivity. First, I become willing to be fully present in the moment. I won't hear/ sense the wisdom of my soul if I'm distracted by old stories my mind replays over and over to keep me tied to the past. I can't hear it if I'm worrying about what might happen in the future. Instead I find it in this moment, no matter what's going on in my life.

Sensing the message is kind of like trying to hear someone in a noisy room—I need to lean in and listen intently. Although it's always available, the message will not try to compete with the noise of my life: my busy schedule, the many text messages or calls on my cell phone. It won't yell over the din of the television, movies or video games. In order to discern the still, small voice within, I'm invited to quiet my life in order to listen. Once I hear it, I'll know that it's the truth. Its message is one of quiet confidence, filling me with a sense of calm purpose. I feel reassured and empowered, with a sure knowing that all is well.

When I let it, my soul guides me toward a happiness greater than I have ever imagined! Shedding the old as I bask in the light of today, I know that change within me is inevitable.

In every given moment I'm at choice. What I think about moves me toward success and happiness or failure and discontent. I ask myself, "What would Love do now?" As I bask in the glow of the greatest Love of all, I sense my answer, finding that it's possible to accept the present circumstance just as it is—without finding it wrong—and in doing so I release my old, habitual reactions. My expectation is that things will work out. I don't need to figure it out or control what will happen; I only know that it will work out. Instead of immediately inserting my opinion, I take a moment to listen . . . really listen, to the voice of wisdom that is within me. Only then do I speak or act, taking my cue from the Presence that knows only truth and love.

I can't ever be separate from the voice of my own inner wisdom— it's impossible! I am a spiritual being, created from the peace, power and presence of the greatest Love of all. It lives and moves through me, bringing its presence to the world in a way that expresses *as me*. It's not just *available* to me—it *invites* a connection that is ongoing and personal. When I'm willing to avail myself of the secret I will sense it, know that it's true and follow its divine lead.

~

I make space to hear the secret . . . the gift of divine wisdom . . . the whisper of truth . . . the beauty of who I am. Then I know what to do.

My Love is a Blessing

Divine Love is alive and awake, fully present in every aspect of my life. It is who I am, expressing as me. At the moment of creation I became the Creator's expression of love, free to show up in my own unique way. As I grow from the ups and downs of my life, the beauty of who I am is fostered. Who I am is a beautiful thing, even when it doesn't look like it through my very human eyes.

As I awaken to my spiritual essence and learn to more fully express who I am, the Beloved constantly holds me in a relationship that is personal and sacred. With each choice that I make, the Beloved is right in the middle of it—a divine set-up orchestrated to get my attention so that I might know the sweetness and the power of my worth. Messages come from a loving universe. The breeze whispers, "Can you feel me? I notice you. You matter to me." The sun reminds me that I have my own light to shine. The beauty of nature pours itself into me, praising me so that I'll remember I am praiseworthy.

Sometimes I feel the weight of the human condition, with all of our vulnerable brokenness. With a need to soothe myself, I wrap my arms around me and gently rock, as if I'm calming a frightened child. As I feel the warmth of Divine Love move into the rhythm of my softness, I feel a comfort that's palpable . . . alive . . . purposeful.

Gratefully, I send that comfort out into the world. I pray,

> Dear Infinite One,
> You created us out of your Love. You hold us forever in
> your Compassion. You invite us to live in your Peace. You
> did it by planting your seed in our hearts so that we will
> remember that we came from you . . . you live as us . . . we
> are your blessed ones. Today, my prayer is that, no matter
> what's going on around us or within us, we remember
> who we are.

In my prayer I remember that I can make a difference. I am Love's
great gift, just as I am. My life and my love blesses the world.

⁓

Divine Love is fully present in my life, as me. Today I
share it, knowing my life and love bless the world.

Chapter 4

I Am a Powerful Creator

WHAT I BELIEVE carries a lot of weight! My beliefs become true for me through spiritual law. Spiritual laws are much like physical laws—they act automatically and are predictable.

Just like the physical laws of gravity, buoyancy, aerodynamics, and electricity, spiritual laws act the same for everyone: the object falls no matter who drops it; the light goes on no matter who flips the switch. Likewise, the power of our thoughts sets in motion the circumstances of our lives, irrespective of who is thinking it. Spiritual laws go hand in hand with free will—our freedom of choice.

Understanding the laws offers me an understanding of why my life is the way it is and an opportunity to head it in a new direction. A shift in consciousness occurs when I embrace the awakening to the truth that I am a powerful creator. It allows me to take responsibility for *what is,* and if I want my life to change, I know that I'm the one who can do it.

My Beliefs are Powerful

My beliefs set into motion the spiritual Law of Cause and Effect—what I believe becomes true for me. Cause is the thought/belief that I plant in the fertile soil of my mind—it doesn't matter whether it's positive or negative. The thought is acted upon automatically, just as soil automatically grows a plant. The effect is the resulting experience which mirrors the thought that I planted. The good news is that once I change the thought I plant (cause) the result (effect) will reflect that change.

For example, if I wake up in the morning and I don't feel like going to work, I have a choice. I can brood, "I don't want to go to work." That thought, and the negative feelings behind it, is acted upon by the creative process of the Law of Cause and Effect. The result will most likely be a less-than-satisfying work day. However, I can choose a different experience! I can inwardly announce, "I intend to have a good day! I'll look for things to be grateful for starting this minute, including my toothbrush and running water to brush my teeth. I'll smile and look for what's right about my work day. My day will be brighter because my attitude is brighter!" After my seed of positivity is planted, I nurture it throughout my day by remembering my intention. The result/effect will be a day of optimism, no matter what the circumstances. I'll begin to realize just how powerful I am!

Spiritual laws are a gift given to us by Divine Creation, through which we co-create our lives with a universe that is attentive and intelligent. If you have a situation in your life that is less than desirable, don't be discouraged! As you make a conscious decision to change the way you think about it, the vibration of your new choice is noticed and acted upon by that same intelligent universe, alive and tuned into you as if you were the only person around. It then begins to create circumstances that correspond to your fresh, uplifting thoughts.

In every moment you are one decision away from living a completely different life. You are the only one who will decide how you'll perceive the moment, which affects how you'll respond to it. Once you've made a conscious decision to see it from a positive perspective, everything that happens after that will be your new actions that will point your life in a new direction. The power of your choice is real. Your life is a big responsibility, a reminder to choose well.

~

Knowing that my beliefs become true for me through spiritual law is a reminder to choose well.

I'm an Impressive Manifestor

When I take to heart the simple and yet remarkable truth that I have within me the same power that runs the universe, it's cause for reflection. As an impressive manifestor I make things happen! Co-creating my life with a friendly universe that says yes to my thoughts, feelings, beliefs and actions is a huge responsibility. I have free will. No one forces me to think a certain way. This leads to some questions:

Am I willing to understand why my life is what it is today and take responsibility for it?

Am I open to changing my focus and altering my attitude in order to shift the circumstances in my life?

Do I believe that I have the power to invite the happiness, fulfillment, and abundance the universe stands ready to give me? If so, how do I do it?

My answers encourage me to own my happiness. I no longer need to be a slave to external circumstances. In a challenging situation I may ask, "How will I be a conscious creator in this situation? How can I move through it well, knowing that my choices create my tomorrows?" I make my choices from the strength and wisdom within me, the part of me that knows what to do. It's much easier to live with the choice I make because it's *mine.*

When I look back at the life I had before I knew the power of my own thinking, I do so gently. I did the best I could with the consciousness I had at the time. Sometimes my best worked in the situation and sometimes my best wasn't very effective. Sometimes I barely tried. The human condition is one of huge variations and sometimes there are days when my best is minimal. The human experience is filled with highs and lows.

Today when I try hard and give it my all, and still my plans don't pan out, I let myself off the hook. I think, "Okay, it didn't work. I gave it my best try, seeing it from every angle, not giving up, and in spite of everything it didn't work. I can beat myself up for time wasted and all the things I must have done wrong, or I can realize there's something better for me ahead. It's time to gather all that I learned from that last endeavor and move on. I'm ready to start again!"

I really am a co-creator with a universe that stands ready to bring me to my highest happiness and success. It's what happens in my head that often stops me. So many times my fears and self-judgment created limits which had absolutely nothing to do with reality! I don't regret it, though, as those memories let me know how far I've come. It really is one step at a time.

Understanding the truth of my power opens the floodgates, allowing the abundance of the universe to enter every area of my life. My power no longer belongs to anyone or anything else— instead it's standing tall within me! Does it feel good? You bet it does!

～

The abundance of the universe flows through every area of my life, all the time. I create my life from the limitless potential within me.

I Am Always Creating

Life is fluid. Change is always in process. What a wonderful thing to know that my powerful thoughts can alter its course. What will I choose? To believe that things will get better opens the door to new possibilities. To believe that I am worth happiness opens the door to abundance in every area of my life. My choices are creative change agents, so I choose wisely.

As I practice seeing the best in every situation, I begin to see evidence of change. I see it when someone makes a critical remark and I don't automatically become defensive or take it personally, as I would have done in the past. I notice my life changing when a new friendship comes into my life, a bit of unexpected income comes my way, or I find myself feeling grateful just to be alive.

I'm part of the natural cycle of transformation. I do my part through changing the way I see myself and the world, and behind the scenes the Universe is doing its part, acting on my behalf through the creative power of my thinking. Then voila! A happier, more fulfilled life has manifested because I've changed! It's much like the chrysalis nurtures a caterpillar, providing a means for transformation as the caterpillar becomes the butterfly. Within my conscious, everyday choices, I provide the means for my own transformation, nurturing my potential with faith and joyful expectancy. I set the stage for the becoming of who I truly am, a magnificent expression of the greatest Love of all!

~

*Every time I choose to see my life through the eyes
of hope and possibility, I create a life that's
happy and fulfilled.*

Choosing Gratitude and Creating Abundance

Have you ever looked back at a time that was full of pain and fear, only to realize it was one of your greatest blessings? If you're in the middle of a great big ol' challenge right now, wouldn't it be wonderful to know that someday you were going to look back on it with gratitude? It seems so hard to trust that there is a big picture while we're in the middle of it. Why don't we relax into the wisdom of our soul and follow its guidance, knowing that the One that's guiding us sees the big picture of our life and knows what it's doing?

Right now most of the world is terrified about money. I wonder, if we were to step back from the fear all around us and look at it from the perspective of the big picture . . . the sure knowing that all is well . . . would we see it in a new light? I bet we would!

The present moment is a grand opportunity for all of us to let go of our human fear and rush into the embrace of the greatest Love of all, just waiting to envelop us in peace and from there lead us to the abundance that is our truth. We are beyond limitation. Divine guidance is within us, inviting us to see the world anew. We need only pay attention and follow its lead.

For many, our spiritual essence is our best kept secret. When we awaken to our truth, we understand that our circumstances don't need to change for us to be peaceful. Instead we can calm our frightened human self by tapping into the peace that we already are.

At present the whole world seems to be filled with thoughts of scarcity and lack. Responsible for our own life, we are the one who can turn those thoughts around. We can't make a change unless we are aware that change needs to be made in the first place. Today is ripe with spiritual possibilities, a glorious chance to go back to the basics, hunkering down with the God of our understanding.

Just like the other periods of crisis in our lives, we may just look back at today and be grateful for it! Wouldn't it be fantastic to have millions of people ultimately say, "My financial adversity became a blessing because in it I found a closer walk with a God that's personal to me. In it I discovered me!"

It's all about our attitude. In this very minute we are birthing our tomorrows. But how to quit being afraid? We can begin by blessing our fear, for it may be our avenue to healing. It's our pathway to inner comfort and guidance . . . our personal relationship with our soul.

It's really important not to deny our feelings and the underlying beliefs and experiences which brought them to the surface. Our soul will remind us that we will always be okay and those uncomfortable feelings are not to be avoided; they are part of the journey. When I first discovered that God was real, and I was really, really afraid, I found that I could bring my weepy, cringing, doubting self straight to the Beloved. In its patient, loving way, I was received with gentle acceptance. I found, through experience, that I could trust the God of my understanding. My fear was held in love until I was able to accept it as a sacred part of me. I quit running away from it and instead became willing to move through it.

The willingness to move through our panic and alarm is pivotal to opening up to our abundance. Sometimes it becomes a habit to be frightened, so we're paralyzed by it without even realizing why. We've been afraid for so long we don't know how to be unafraid! For some, fear also gets us off the hook. We say, "I'm frightened," and use it as an excuse to stay stuck in the same box we've been in for years, settling for much less than the joy that awaits. Our ego would have us stay in that tiny fear box and never move forward, doing its best to keep us safe, but at the same time we stay trapped.

Once we awaken, we can do something about it. Our prayer involves the willingness to move through our fear and to step into being all we can be. It's a big step, scary in itself! And yet there is a part of us gently urging us forward. Sensing our shift in consciousness, the universe opens up doors to success wherein we will be bigger and more than we ever thought we would be! We're not here as spiritual beings having a human experience to play small.

Because we create through the power of our thinking, we are in charge of our own happiness. We were gifted free will by a God that lovingly gave us the freedom to think and move and be whoever we choose to be. No matter what we believe, the response is, "And so it is," giving us the result of that belief. Fear is a mighty creator. If we stay in fear around money, "And so it is," gives us more to be afraid of. Scarcity, lack and limitation are the norm because our focus is on what we *don't* have.

In my personal experience, I have found that the polar opposite of fear is gratitude, because gratitude focuses us on what we *do* have. Giving thanks for everything, from the shampoo that cleans our hair to the blanket that covers us as we sleep, brings about more to be grateful for, including financial abundance! What we think in one area of our life affects every area of our life. Our appreciation for the rain watering the earth and the warmth of the sun are just as apt to bring prosperity our way as checking the internet for job openings. The universe doesn't pay attention to big or small; it only knows that we're feeling grateful, and it creates from our gratitude. Its natural response is to send more goodness our way so we can continue to feel grateful. Life then gives us more to feel good about—it's a powerful cycle of abundance! It's up to us to decide what we want and at the same time, to appreciate what we already have. Staying in gratitude feels good! We feel an undercurrent of power that frees us to move beyond our old limitations to make new choices and take new actions.

For many, a new action step is financial giving. In times of financial fear it's critically important, especially if we think we don't have it to give. Remember that our beliefs are creative, and if our belief is that we don't have enough to give, we get to be right; there won't be enough. It is imperative to find something to give if we want to turn our finances around.

The first step is changing our perception of giving. As our faith grows, we give with an attitude of gratitude just for the joy of sharing from our abundance, even if we can't see abundance in our life at the moment. If this is you, you might be asking, how do I begin? Right where you are is a great place to start!

If you're on a fixed income that seems stretched to the limit, you can still give. If you decide not to buy your weekly latte, your income was just raised by $2.50. Buying generic products also increases your income, and you now have something to give! Try looking for unexpected income in your life, those areas of abundance you may never have noticed before. In doing so, you stretch your consciousness, which in turn brings about prosperity. Here's how it works:

- You expect to pay $40 for jeans and find that they are on sale for $30, that's $10 unexpected income.
- You go out to eat and your friend picks up the tab, "Thank you!" That's unexpected income.
- At the grocery store your favorite cereal is two-for-one. The money you saved is unexpected income.
- Your car insurance goes down. The amount of the reduction is unexpected income.
- A coupon for a product you routinely buy shows up in the mail. The coupon is unexpected income.
- The price of gas goes down. The amount saved on your purchase of gas is unexpected income.
- When you find a nickel on the sidewalk or in the folds of your couch, that's unexpected income, too!

Every time you recognize your unexpected income as abundance, you give 10% of it (or 5% or 2%, whatever works for you). If you're giving 10% and you saved $1, you give a dime. If you saved $4.50

you give $0.45. If you received an unexpected check for $100 you give $10. Watch what happens when you recognize and are grateful for your good, "I give with joy because *I have it to give!*" No longer are you a victim of "I don't have enough money." You are now in a whole new energy field of prosperity, with the vibration of "I am abundant!" to which the universe says, "And so it is; you are abundant!" and more abundance comes your way. It doesn't so much matter how much you give, but that you give with gratitude and joy because *you have it to give.*

You get to decide where to give; someplace that has meaning for you. Many give to their church or spiritual home, others give to their favorite charity. If you've started volunteering, that often becomes a great place to give because you're invested in its success. Just as it feels good to give of your time and expertise, financial giving also benefits everyone, especially *you.*

Our minds are like fertile gardens. Ask yourself, "What seed am I planting?" If money is on your mind today, consider, "Am I planting the seed of gratitude or the seed of fear? Is my result abundance or lack?" Remember that you can plant new seeds, starting today. Pretend you are a master gardener, and let these steps nurture the seeds of your tomorrow:

- Without judgment, become aware of your feelings, actions, reactions, and choices about money.
- Take any negative feelings straight to the God of your understanding. Be honest with yourself as you rest in its unconditional love.
- Cultivate a prayer for the willingness to move through your negativity in order to move toward your full potential.
- Begin to be grateful for everything in your life.
- Stretch your prosperity consciousness by looking for unexpected income.
- Begin to give from that unexpected income, no matter

what the amount.

- Let your attitude of gratitude direct your choices and next steps in the area of prosperity.

Your new perspective brings you into alignment with your true essence. It deepens your personal relationship with your own inner strength. Once you understand how truly loved you are, you automatically become grateful for everything, and the whole world supports you. It is a natural outcome of your love affair with the Divine. Trusting the big picture, you give birth to the unborn possibility of your limitless abundance, beginning with the first thought.

~

With gratitude, I enthusiastically say YES to the limitless abundance of the universe, knowing I'm meant to live a life that's joyous, prosperous and free.

Creating My Happiness

Many of us were taught to put the needs of others before our own. Once I discovered that God was real, I learned to think a new way. The Beloved told me that I'm worthy of my own happiness. Then when I give my attention to another, it comes from an inner feeling of joy instead of a sense of duty.

First I needed to learn what made *me* happy. I had been so busy getting through my day, doing what needed to be done, that I didn't really pay attention to what I was enjoying. I started by being fully present in each moment, as much as possible. I asked, "Is what I'm doing right now making me happy? If so, why? If not, why not?" I asked the same question about the people I was with, "Is this person adding to my happiness? If so, why? If not, why not?" The same was true of what was going on in my own head—were my thoughts adding to my happiness? If so, why? If not, why not? I started to keep a journal about what made me happy. I also started to consciously make time for the activities, people and thoughts that brought happiness to my life. As I did so, I began to let go of the activities, people and thoughts that weren't making me happy. It was life changing! It took practice, perseverance and courage. My inner cheerleader kept encouraging me because I was worthy of my own happiness.

Once I become aware of what made happy and made time for it, my life automatically became more joyous and fulfilled. Why? Because my beliefs, thoughts, and feelings are creative. The Law of Attraction is all about feelings! Our feelings create a vibrational field around us that acts as a magnet, calling to us people, circumstances and events that are on the same magnetic field. If our vibrational field is optimistic, we will attract people and situations who are relishing in the goodness of life. If we are feeling discouraged or angry, we will attract people and circumstances that match our negativity. My life automatically began to change because I had changed! I was now hanging out in a vibrational field of happiness and self-worth.

Knowing what makes me happy points me in the direction of more happiness. If I'm struggling with a loved one's behavior and know I can't control their life (as much as I want to), what I can do is take care of myself. I ask, "What can I do this minute to make *me* happy?" Will I listen to a favorite song, take a short walk, laugh out loud at a sitcom rerun, read an uplifting article, go for a bike ride, call a friend, or pay special attention to my pet? My happiness belongs to me—another person's happiness (or lack of happiness) belongs to them. In consciously choosing happiness, I become a role model for possibility just by showing up in the world. Today I keep my "Happiness" list handy and when life seems to be turned upside down, I choose from it and take action.

The choice to be happy belongs to me. When I'm happy and think about my loved one who's struggling, I'm able to send them upbeat, optimistic energy because that's where I'm hanging out.

My positive energy is much more helpful to them than my wish to fix them because I somehow think they're broken. My optimistic outlook not only helps me, it positively affects the world.

⁓

I consciously choose happiness in my life, creating a space for even more happiness to show up.

Behind the Mask

I used to hide behind a happy-face mask, pretending that life was wonderful when it wasn't. I was so busy being what others wanted me to be that I forgot who I was. When I discovered the God of my understanding the mask came off. Slowly my own thoughts, my own voice, my own truth surfaced. I realized I wasn't born to fit into someone else's expectations—my job is to live my life as me!

It's okay to be who I am, no matter what the situation and who I'm with. Every time I practice being true to myself I send a clear message to the universe about what I like and what I stand for. In return I attract more of what I like into my experience. Living an ambivalent life gets ambivalent results, so clarity is a really good thing! I ask myself these questions: What's important to me? What do I stand for? What values guide my actions? What am I attracted to? What do I avoid? When have I set important boundaries with others and with myself? What did I learn from the experience?

When I taught little kids I had them put their hand over their opposite shoulder and pat themselves on the back for a job well done, and everything counted! As I stay true to myself in each situation—no matter how it turns out–I pat myself on the back for doing it. Taking off the mask honors me, and a bit of self-recognition is in order!

⁓

Today I remove the mask that hides who I am. I find my voice, write my own script and live my life as me!

Creating from Forgiveness

You may have heard the story of the teacher who asked each of her students to bring a plastic bag and a sack of potatoes to school. For every person they refuse to forgive, they chose a potato, wrote the person's name on it, and put it in the plastic bag. Some of their bags were quite heavy!

They were then told to carry this bag everywhere they went for one week, putting it beside their bed at night and on the car seat when driving. Naturally, the condition of the potatoes deteriorated to a nasty smelly slime. This is a great metaphor for the price I pay for holding onto my pain and negativity. Too often I think of forgiveness as a gift to the other person, when clearly it's for me.

There are many reasons to forgive. Among them is the damage that non-forgiveness does to me. Non-forgiveness calls for a hefty dose of resentment, anger and blame. The energy of my negativity shows up in every area of my life, just as if I were carrying around that stinky bag of potatoes. It's just not worth it. Forgiveness is one of the greatest gifts I can give myself.

What Life does for me it must do through me. Life is always at work and is limited only by my beliefs, thoughts, feelings, words and actions. Only I can decide that I'm tired of carrying around that sack of rotting potatoes and am I ready to create from forgiveness instead of resentment and pain. Finally I realize that I'm ready to value myself enough to forgive because I'm worth a life of happiness.

~

I value myself enough to let go of past hurts and resentments. In forgiveness, I'm free to accept every good life has to offer!

I Was Born to Live My Dreams

I was created from pure potential—it's at the core of who I am. Living my happiest, best life is my divine calling. As pure potential, I was born with the talents to reach my dreams, bringing my unique gift to the world. Little by little, I've learned to say yes to my life, my potential and my gifts.

I was born in California and have lived there all my life. The first time I drove across the San Francisco Golden Gate Bridge by myself was during ministerial school. I was in my late 50s. Before that other people were behind the wheel. The significance of being the one behind the wheel brought tears to my eyes as I realized that a whole new world was opening up. My job was to keep saying yes to it. Age makes no difference. Saying yes is what counts.

My dreams continue to unfold because I keep saying yes to what feels right and no to what doesn't. I'm creating a space for my dreams to come true because I'm standing tall in what's important to me.

If you're wondering what your happiest life might look like, you might begin by contemplating, "I am open to living my dreams," and then I pay attention. What images show up? What feeling do you have in the pit of your stomach? What thoughts come to the surface? Write it down. Draw pictures. Sit with it again and again.

When you're ready to act on what's been emerging, get quiet and centered, sensing the presence of your own inner wisdom. Ask, "What do I do about it?" The first step will be revealed—for me it's often the next positive thought that surfaces. I take action on that positive thought, even if it doesn't make sense to me. Then I'll stay the course! I'll keep asking, listening, and then taking action, knowing that I co-create my life with the universe. My faith muscle will grow stronger as I have the courage to say yes to my dreams.

You'll get into the groove of letting your happiness become known. You'll start to say yes to what feels right and no to what doesn't, even when people are disappointed in you because you didn't make the choice they wanted you to make. It's *your* life . . . *your* dreams . . . *your* happiness. Owning it is your divine calling.

⁓

I am meant to live my dreams. I have the courage to make them happen.

Mental Sunshine

Because I'm a powerful creator, I can take any moment in time, change my perspective, and find something to be grateful for. Because it's really hard to be unhappy and grateful at the same time, in that moment I'm releasing the negative cloud over my head and creating mental sunshine instead! Gratitude promotes mental, emotional and physical health. It also opens the doorway to serenity, a career that makes me glad to go to work, meaningful relationships and any other desire on my wish list.

I used to wonder how all that worked. Then I learned about how I co-create with the universe with my own thinking. Pretty amazing! Because thought is creative, what I'm thinking right now is creating my tomorrows. If I'm focusing on what's wrong in my life, I'm creating more sorrows for the future. This can show up as a back ache, a job lay-off or disappointing relationships. Knowing my life is created by where I put my mental and emotional focus, wouldn't I choose to concentrate on what I want? That's where gratitude comes in!

For instance, if I'm sitting in traffic, in a waiting room, standing in line, or on hold on the phone, instead of being impatient, I choose a color and think of as the many things I appreciate that happen to be that color. If I choose the color blue, things I appreciate may include my favorite blue coffee cup, the blue sky overhead, my comfy old blue shirt and my neon blue toothbrush. If I'm at a stop light I look around and notice a child with a blue jacket or the blue van in the next lane, and I find myself silently wishing them well on their journey. The practice of appreciation provides an opportunity to create my sunshiny tomorrows from what's right in front of me, no matter what's going on around me. All it takes is a focus adjustment!

~

Today I become an ambassador for mental sunshine,
changing my life one gratitude at a time.

What Would You Do?

In the fall of 1998, a few months after I discovered that God was real, I was in a workshop when the question was asked, "What would you do if you could do anything you wanted and be guaranteed success?" Without thinking I wrote, "I'd change careers." Then I gasped! How could I even think of leaving my teaching career? All I ever wanted to do was teach children. Caught off guard by my own answer, I didn't tell anyone what I had written, but I also didn't forget about it.

That question was clearly the work of the Beloved, planting a seed of possibility. By the end of that school year I left my 20-year teaching career, and everyone thought I was crazy! To the many who asked why, my answer was, "I'm following a dream." When they asked, "What dream?" my response was, "I don't know." Then they really thought I had gone over the deep end. But somehow it was okay not to know because by this point I'd learned that the Beloved was trustworthy, and I was following Love's lead.

My faith allowed me to move forward without having any idea of what was around the corner. It was scary—really scary! But something within me knew that I was doing the right thing.

That was the beginning of my journey to becoming a minister, an international speaker and a writer. I was being led toward careers that makes my heart sing!

So the question is, "What would you do if you could do anything you wanted and be guaranteed success?" You are a powerful creator! Don't play small. Don't worry about what people would say or all the reasons why it wouldn't work. You don't even need to know the end result. All you need to do is say yes to the next step. Just think about it. Then say yes! Your life is waiting.

~

Today I say yes to life by opening myself to new and exciting possibilities!

The Power of My Positive Thought

Positivity rules! One positive thought, affirmed and believed, disarms negativity and shines a light in a bright new direction. As I move through my day I contribute to a world that works for everyone by choosing to see and be grateful for what's already working.

I begin each day with positivity in my heart. I notice the beauty of what I see with my own eyes, hear about from others, and imagine in my own mind. How many adults, children and pets will be hugged today, kind words said to another, trash recycled, trees planted, and smiles shared? Just think of the millions who will pray today, reaching out to the God of their understanding, knowing they will be heard.

The vibration of my positive thoughts makes its way to people I don't know and may never meet, but somehow it uplifts their day. What might happen if we *all* focused on what's already right in today's world, knowing that others will feel the energy of our optimism? Lives will change, and together we just might create a world that works for everyone!

~

I create a world that works for everyone by looking through optimistic eyes and positivity in my heart.

Chapter 5

I Am Worthy

I AM WORTHY of a life that's fulfilled and happy. When I create a space for happiness, happiness finds me. It may not show up in a way that I expected, but it will find me nonetheless—enjoying a good book, the fragrance of coffee brewing, eating a meal I enjoy, laughing at my pet's antics, awakening from a good night's sleep, giving myself credit for taking the trash out or making the phone call I've been putting off. I ask myself how I can pay forward the good feelings that are within me in the moment, so I send a card to a shut in, a birthday or sympathy card where needed, or put a wayward shopping cart back where it belongs. Each reminds me that as I move in a positive direction, I change. I notice what's right in the world and jump right in to join it!

I Am Worthy of Happiness

My beliefs underscore my perceptions of life, guiding my relationships, financial choices, and self-esteem. If I believe that life circumstances or other people have power over my happiness, I'm falling prey to a belief that I'm powerless. Relying on others to make me happy is frustrating and futile. How are they supposed to know what will make me happy in this instant when half the time I don't even know what I need? Am I going to ask them to give up their own needs and dreams for mine?

Learning to own my happiness is empowering—I'm the one who learns to recognize what I want and go after it. I'm the one who will come to realize that I'm worthy of the time, focused attention and dedicated practice it takes to create a life that's happy and free. It's my decision to turn away from negativity and choose to see the simple goodness that exists in the world. My faith grows as I let go of drama and embrace peace, beginning with what takes place in my own mind. It really does begin with me, and today happiness is my choice.

~

I own my happiness. I'm worthy of making the changes that allow happiness into my life.

I Am Worthy of Inner Peace

Even though it's wonderful when things are going my way, my inner peace isn't dependent upon what's happening around me. I can still choose the path of peace when things are out of whack. I can step away from a conversation filled with blame and gossip. I no longer need to dive into the drama of a situation or fight to control those around me. I can choose to let go of the turmoil and set a new course toward the peace I deserve instead.

Because inner peace is up to me, I take charge of what I can control. If I usually run late to work, I can set the alarm and get up earlier because my peace of mind has become a priority. Then I congratulate myself for doing it! I ask, "What else can I do to start my day on a positive note?" and then I take action on it. Just one change makes a huge difference! Every single time I make a change on my own behalf, the universe hears, "I'm worthy of inner peace," and more peace-filled situations come my way.

It takes practice, determination and courage to let go of the people, situations and events that keep peace at bay—the relationship that's no longer in my best interest, the habit I've had for years but is now detrimental to the life I want to live, or the fear that I won't be good enough to do the things I want to do. Shaking myself loose from the circumstances that are no longer in my best interests is a gift I give myself.

～

Choosing peace is a way of living through the choices I make daily. My inner peace is up to me.

I Am Worthy of Being Honest with Myself

It wasn't until I started Al-Anon that I learned to be honest with myself. For such a long time I'd pretended that everything was fine when it wasn't. Walking through the doors of a 12-step program to admit that my life was a mess was scary, but the fear didn't last. I was with others who were in the process of doing the same thing, and no one curled up and died when they admitted that they needed help. Then I discovered that self-honesty was liberating! What a relief to finally tell the truth! Soon I had a sponsor and I began to be honest with her, and then with others. Bit by bit, I learned to tell the truth, standing tall in who I am instead of pretending to be someone I'm not. My self-esteem and self-respect grew.

In the process of promoting honesty, I realized that what I say and do in the company of others is one thing, and what goes on when I'm alone can be quite another. Because I have the undivided attention of a universe that's always saying yes to me, it hears and acts on the unspoken self-criticism that sometimes yells loudly in my head. It was time to take stock of what I was listening to. Within my mind are many voices—the voices of fear, judgment, resentment and guilt as well as the voices of reason, intellect, self-will and past experience. Within my heart there is one voice—the voice of love, compassion, wisdom and interconnectedness. Learning to listen to the voice that's right for me takes conscious attention and dedicated practice.

The practice of being honest with myself has helped me accept all of me. I no longer need to pretend that life is perfect and that I have everything handled. It's quite okay to be accept that my human experience is often messy. Being open and honest with myself allows for self-compassion in my vulnerability and self-love in my acceptance of life, just as it is. Today I honor all of me, messes included!

~

Being honest with myself honors all of me,
including the ups and downs of my very human life.

I Am Worthy of Feeling My Emotions

Life is full of contrasts from which I learn to know myself. How am I to appreciate light if I've never known darkness? How can I realize the joy of success if I've never experienced disappointment, frustration and failure? My emotions become the conduit through which I understand myself in a deeper, more compassionate way. As a spiritual being having a human experience, it's time to honor the feelings and emotions that are part of the human experience package . . . all of them. I am peace *and* anger, compassion *and* resentment, clarity *and* confusion, courage *and* fear, self-respect *and* guilt. I needn't hide from who I am!

For many of us, it's uncomfortable to even admit that we have negative feelings such as anger, guilt, fear and judgment. Many of us were taught as children that anger is wrong and that our fears are unreasonable. We were taught to avoid any strong feelings, especially negative ones. Today those tendencies may linger. We may not have allowed ourselves the time and space to feel the feelings and shed the tears that we've held back for so long. Instead we try to avoid them, numbing ourselves with hours of television, Internet use, gambling, drinking, shopping or gossiping about others so that we don't have to think about our own life.

While we do our best to put on a happy face, our emotions are just under the surface, stored in our subconscious mind. For instance, we may say that we don't have anger, but anger shows itself when the dishwasher breaks, or someone disagrees with us, or we're stuck in traffic. The anger is there all along. It doesn't go away just because we pretend it isn't there. Instead it has been warehoused in our subconscious mind, waiting to be acknowledged, sometimes for years. In our pursuit of happiness we declare our affirmation, "I am joyous and free!" but our affirmation must make its way through our subconscious mind, where it gets bogged down in our unexpressed anger. Then we wonder why our life isn't changing. *What we resist persists.* If we resist the anger or any other negative feeling, it only gets driven down deeper into our subconscious mind and comes up more intensely later, when we least expect it. As long as we ignore it, we will continue to feel the effects of its presence.

What if we gave up the idea that our negative emotions are wrong and accepted them as a normal and natural part of our human experience? What if we make a conscious decision to welcome all of our emotions, inviting them to be fully felt so that they can then subside naturally?

Try this: Find time to be alone or with a trusted friend or spiritual counselor. Become quiet, centered and still, open to loving and honoring yourself in a new way. Then invite any emotion/feeling to come forward. If anger arises, invite it to speak. If fear arises, ask it to come forward to make itself known. Knowing that you are safe, that those negative emotions are simply uncomfortable sensations in your body, allow each to be felt. You may picture it as an angry or fearful child who wants you to know how it feels. Maybe it's a reflection of you as a child. Isn't it time to let yourself be heard? Let it stand and speak, and invite it to share whatever message it's been waiting to tell you.

The process may become difficult, but it's important to stay with it, to give that emotion your full attention. If you need to cry, then cry; let it out! Stay the course, whether it takes a few minutes or an hour; just let it continue. When it appears that your emotion has completed its task of being noticed, felt and accepted, ask, "Is there anything else?"

Make sure you offer it all the time and attention it needs. Thank it before saying goodbye for now as you release it. Then stay in the quiet until you have once again become centered, filled with the presence of the Love that created you. Let the Beloved's divine love wash over you and fill you, holding you until you realize how gently and unconditionally you are loved, exactly as you are.

You may want to follow up this session by journaling about it. You don't need to be a great writer—just let the words flow. You may want to draw pictures in your journal with crayons or colored pencils: What did your emotion look like as the process began and then again at the end, once it had been felt, honored and released? Don't worry about what your drawings look like—the power is in the process and expression, not the finished product.

Journaling is an important spiritual practice which can result in a growing ability to accept yourself with new-found understanding and self-compassion. By knowing that no one else will ever see it, you are free to write or draw your innermost thoughts. You may even find that as you write, more emotions will surface. Ask, "What do you want me to know?" and write about the messages your emotions bring forward.

Once you become open to feeling your emotions, you will get into the flow of non-resistance, where emotions are noticed, felt, and then released on an ongoing basis as a normal and natural part of your life. No more hiding from yourself! You will allow the past to be where it can do the most good—in the past, because you are no longer carrying it around in unresolved emotions.

Now when you declare your affirmation, "I am joyous and free!" Life will respond by sending you experiences, people and situations that support your affirmation one hundred percent!

~

I accept and appreciate every aspect of myself, including my most challenging emotions.

I Am Worthy of Setting Boundaries

There was a time when I thought setting boundaries was unkind. Disagreeing with others made me uncomfortable. I wanted people to like me. I wanted everything to be peaceful. So I looked at it from what I thought was their point of view and found many reasons to back down. I was so used to putting myself in the other person's shoes that I didn't know how to stand in my own. I ended up in the middle of drama instead of the peace I wanted to create.

I finally learned that if I accept poor behavior I'm not helping anyone. If I allow someone to speak to me unkindly, not only will I feel horrible, I'm helping to foster unkindness in them. If I make excuses for a loved one's irresponsibility, I'm not being honest with myself or with them. When I don't set limits on what I will and will not accept, my happiness is at the mercy of those around me.

Behaviors have consequences, and the sooner we deal with them the better off we all are. Giving others the dignity of being responsible for their own behavior honors them and it honors me.

Even if they're raving mad at me for not seeing it their way and helping them out of the hole they've gotten themselves into, setting boundaries is loving kindness in action.

~

By letting others deal with the consequences of their own behavior, I am honoring them and myself.

I Am Worthy of My Highest Good

Life is what I make of it. The universe stands ready to fulfill my utmost desires once I'm clear about what they are. As I stay focused on the wisdom of my soul, I'm continually guided to my highest good . . . my greatest happiness . . . a life of fulfillment.

When I ask, "How do I start?" my soul answers, "Start where you are. I will meet you there." Each day—and sometimes many times during the day—I seek the advice of the part of me that knows what to do with each situation that's in front of me.

My inner wisdom tells me to stay in gratitude for everything, as gratitude changes my perspective, uplifts every outcome and brings about a shift in consciousness which will send life's goodness my way. When I spend my day looking for reasons to be grateful, I find them everywhere! I'm grateful for the beating of my heart, my breath, the skin that covers and protects my body, and my feet that take me where I want to go. I'm grateful for the shade of a nearby tree, rain on the roof, bees pollinating flowers, bicycle racks and walks through the park.

When I find a reason to be grateful for someone, I tell them. The energy of genuinely praising another is good for everyone, including the person doing the praising—that's me! When I find a reason to praise myself, I do it. It reminds me that I'm worth my own positive energy.

When I look back at my most difficult challenges, I find reasons to be grateful for them, too. Part of that gratitude is the humble compassion I now have for others who are struggling, either with circumstances outside their control or the messes that they've created. When I'm in the presence of someone who has felt defeat, fought to overcome it and finally found their way out of it, I'm uplifted. The same is true about those who have made horrible choices that have caused pain to themselves and others. Just like me, it brings about a depth of humility and understanding that can be felt when they are with another who has erred. In reality, this is all of us—these are all of our stories. They connect us to each other as spiritual beings having a very human experience. Through our difficult experiences we see each other, and for that I am grateful.

My soul gently reminds me to stop complaining that what I have isn't enough. Instead, I'm to get busy and make the most of what I have. With my spiritual awakening, I know that I am much more than the physical reality of what I can see, hear, feel, touch and taste. My life is filled with possibilities my human mind can't even imagine! Instead I tap into my spiritual wisdom. First thing in the morning I listen inwardly for the message of the day. What am I to think, do or be today? Will it be a day of communicating with others, writing, getting errands done, making a difference to someone else, bringing the best of who I am to my work environment? How can I best stay open to the possibilities alive in each circumstance? When I stay tuned to the message of the day, my day not only goes smoothly, it's full and rewarding. When I don't, it's less than satisfying. It's a reminder that the wisdom within me knows what its doing.

As I focus on what's right in my life, I find many ways to move forward! I start from where I am, with what I have, and patiently do what is in front of me. As I take action doors begin to open. There's no limit to where I can go!

~

Putting one foot in front of the other, I start where I am.
My highest good is waiting for me.

I Am Worthy of a Harmonious Life

I want to live a harmonious life, but sometimes the biggest stumbling block is *me*. When I'm afraid to move forward, I can find lots of reasons to stall the process. Even when the time is right I can find every excuse for not starting a project—I'm not sure how to start, I need help and don't want to ask, I don't have the energy, I need to finish my other project, the task is too big, blah, blah, blah. Whereas the task at hand is intended to enrich my life, my fear brings it to a screeching halt. Although I want to bring harmony into my life, my growing disharmony caused by my excuses is brewing, showing up in my body as insomnia, an inability to focus, emotional eating, an aching back and catching the latest cold or flu. The discord in my body tells me that in my procrastination I'm lying to myself.

Why am I fighting so hard to push harmony away when it's the very thing I desire? For me it often has to do with control, which is a byproduct of fear. Starting something new invites the unknown into the picture. The unknown can be scary! What if it shows up in a way I can't control? Ah, now I know the real reason why I've been putting off taking that first step—it pulls me out of my comfort zone where everything is familiar and predictable.

My comfort zone may be my old friend, but it doesn't necessarily have my best interests at heart. When I look back at all the times that I let fear of leaving my comfort zone stop me, did my life feel harmonious? Not a bit! My comfort zone may have been familiar, but it sure didn't feel very comfortable!

My life isn't going to be harmonious until I allow myself to go with the flow of life's changes. The first step is to become willing to change my mind, remembering the times when I stepped out of the familiar to do what was in front of me. How did it feel? Scary, but it was also filled with a growing sense of I-can-do-it self-worth.

After I discovered that God was real, it got easier because I knew I wasn't alone—within me and all around me the greatest

Love of all supported each step. Do I think it's going to be different this time? No—that same Presence is right where I am.

Harmony takes place when I'm in the flow of life, allowing the changes that present themselves throughout the day. Taking the time to be quiet and feel the presence of the One that adores me, I take a deep breath and begin with the first step, and then the next one, leaving my disharmonious comfort zone far behind as faith and trust take its place.

I say yes to harmony in my mind, in my body and in my life because I'm worth it.

~

Letting go of resistance, I step into the flow of a life that's harmonious, empowering, and free.

I Am Worthy of Being My Own Best Friend

The Beloved is teaching me to become my own best friend. I'm not to say anything to myself that I wouldn't let someone say about my best friend. I'm reminded to acknowledge the things I do well, to speak words that are positive, to hang out with people who uplift me, to engage in activities that are fun, and to be grateful for *me*. I'm enthusiastically given permission to put myself first, to pay attention to what makes me happy, and then I'm gently instructed to take action toward owning my happiness.

Self-kindness heals. When I'm kind to myself I tend to be kind to others. When I'm hurting Love reminds me to be gentle with myself, just as I've been gentle with others. When I make a mistake, I do my best to wrap myself in self-kindness, learn from the situation, make amends if needed and then let myself off the hook. My sense of worthiness grows.

With each new understanding, my relationship with myself deepens. Every time I treat myself gently—telling myself that I'm okay—self-understanding and compassion take root. When I choose a positive thought instead of falling back on my old negativity, I create a space for change.

The Beloved reminds me that I'm worth the dedicated practice of conscious transformation. Becoming my own best friend has helped me see myself in a new light—I'm not only worth the change that comes with transformation, I'm worth every happiness! Just ask my best friend!

~

I'm my own best friend, filled with self-kindness and self-compassion. I treat myself gently as I learn and grow, knowing I'm worthy of every happiness!

I Am Worthy of Saying Yes to Me

Spring is a time of awakening, one new blade of grass at a time. That tiny shoot of bright green hides in the winter, unnoticed by the humans and animals walking on the soil above its resting place. All the while it has been growing and maturing unseen within its cradle of earth, nurtured by soil and water until the warmth of the sun lures it out of hiding.

Just like that blade of grass breaking through the surface of the soil to live the life it was meant to live, I am invited to a greater awareness of the beauty of who I am. There is a river of never-ending creation that flows through me, with joy and fulfillment as its intended result. I know I'm on the path when I'm so caught up in an activity that all of a sudden I look at the clock and wonder, "Where did the time go?" It may be writing, taking photos, listening to music, talking with a friend, reading a book, enjoying a hobby or walking in nature. Whatever it is, my life is changed when I include it in my life on a regular basis.

By consciously learning to notice, value and appreciate what pleases me, I'm saying yes to me. The universe notices my joy and responds by giving me more reasons to be happy. When I say yes to the activities I enjoy and actually make time for them, I'm birthing a new sense of self-appreciation and self-love. Once again, the universe responds by giving me more reasons to value myself. The "proof" can show up as a genuine compliment, an easy recovery from an illness, a healed relationship, a new friend, an inspirational idea or the realization that the old grievance I've been carrying around is now gone. That's the way it works! It begins by honoring myself and it grows from there. Just as the blade of grass grows tall, with strong roots holding it in place, the strong roots of my newfound self-worth give me the needed strength to grow into the person I want to be.

~

Every day I incorporate activities that make me happy.

I'm worth saying yes to me!

Chapter 6

I Am Capable

NOW THAT I'VE AWAKENED to and developed a personal relationship with the God of my understanding, my whole outlook on life has opened up. No matter what has happened in my past, today is an invitation to recognize the sacred beauty within me that has the power to heal.

At my core is an unconditional Love so great that nothing would cause it to turn away from me. Instead, it has been patiently waiting for me to notice that it has been there all along. Knowing that I co-create my life with a universe that says yes to the energy of my beliefs, thoughts, words and actions, the next step belongs to me.

Making Conscious Choices

One of the greatest gifts I can give myself is to consciously choose where to place my focus. Will I focus on my God or on my problem? Gratitude or victimization? Compassion or resentment? Peace or drama? Self-understanding or self-condemnation?

Every moment is a choice. If I'm invited to an activity I don't really want to attend, I can say no. If I've already said yes and change my mind, I can now say no, I've changed my mind. Period. No need for explanations. If I've said yes, I will attend the activity and then I don't feel comfortable once I'm there, I can leave.

How many times have I been in a conversation that just didn't feel right, but I didn't know how to get out of it? Now I know that if I'm in a discussion that makes me uncomfortable, I can quietly excuse myself. If my mind chatter is negative, I can say no to the chatter and replace it with my favorite affirmation or a list of things to feel grateful about.

Sometimes it's tempting to try to win—win the argument, win the money, the best promotion or the relationship I think I must have. The problem comes when winning goes against what I know is right. I ask myself, "How do I want to feel about this situation when I look back on it? Is it worth going against what my gut is telling me is wrong?" If a feeling of possible regret surfaces, it's my opportunity to choose a new direction now, letting tomorrow's regret slide away today.

In a challenging situation my prayer becomes, "Dear Beloved One, I know that this is somehow a gift from you. I don't need to understand it to accept it. Please help me move through it well." Making the conscious choice to like myself in the situation, I automatically begin to remove negativity. The situation isn't nearly as important as how I move through it.

A shift in consciousness has awakened me. I am capable of making conscious choices in every situation, knowing that the answers I seek are within me, ever available to lead me toward my highest good. What will I choose? I really am a powerful creator, living a life that belongs to me. Today I own my choices, take responsibility for my life, and when I've goofed, I know I can choose again.

~

By making conscious choices, I say yes to my
very best life.

Mistakes as Growing Tools

There's much to be said about living long enough to make lots of mistakes and then growing from them. It leads to new perspectives and priorities and a greater awareness of who I am today. Can you imagine still having the mentality you had when you were a teenager, freshly out of childhood, trying to figure out who you are and how you fit into the world? Who will be my friends? Will they like me? How do I fit in? Do they have the same values? What are my values, anyway? Teenagers tend to learn what's important to them by trying things out, wondering what will happen and hoping their parents never find out.

In the process of growing and maturing I discover what's important to me in each stage of my life. I can listen to those around me and be guided by what I see, hear and read, but until I experience life it's all just a bunch of good ideas . . . someone else's ideas. So I stumble along, falling down often and picking myself up. Every so often the falling down is pretty messy and is certainly humbling. I muck around in my own frailties, sometimes for years, until I decide "Enough!" I discover that I have a choice about staying in my stuck-ness or getting up and moving forward. That's when I decide to pick myself up once again.

Mistakes help me remember that I'm learning . . . traveling into unchartered territory. How can I move forward if I stay tethered to that which I already know? It would be like a teenager sticking with the friends and activities from their childhood years and never trying anything new. It's humbling to own my mistakes and denying them to others can be tempting. However, rejecting their existence sets me up for the negativity of guilt and shame that secrets can bring into my life. Being accountable for my actions is a sign of my growing faith, self-honesty and feeling of self-worth. With my willingness to pick myself up and step out of the darkness, I test the waters of all that's new, letting go of the need to stay in the familiar. Mistakes are the other side of the success coin. Bless them! Through my mistakes, I make my way toward success.

The Beloved's unconditional love helps me learn from my mistakes and stand tall today. I've changed a lot over the course of my lifetime! I'm stronger and wiser now, and for that I'm grateful.

~

Mistakes are my growing tools. I learn from each and am wiser because of them.

Finding Gifts in Adversity

It's easy to love life when things are going well. However, I've discovered that some of my greatest gifts have come as a result of my challenges. I rarely see the gifts right away—sometimes it takes years to realize what I gained as I struggled through a particular circumstance.

Challenges are a normal and natural part of change—it's what I do with them that counts. How often have I spent days stewing about the problem, "This is terrible! Why did it have to happen now, just when my life was looking up? What a mess!" When I'm immersed in, "Isn't it awful?" it leaves no room for solutions. If I would have simply accepted it instead of vehemently resisting it, it could likely have been solved a whole lot sooner. Did I know that then? No. I really do believe we do the best we can with what we know at the time. Now that I know better, I do better. In the scope of my challenges I've learned:

- to stand up for myself;
- to let go when necessary;
- to trust my intuition;
- to trust the flow of the situation so that I can stay open to next steps;
- to have faith that a solution will make itself known
- to turn to prayer, "Help me move through this with grace;"

- that sometimes the problem doesn't even belong to me—my job is to back off;
- that I can be my own hero instead of a victim;
- that I can ask others for help;
- that the difficulty may be heading me in a brand new, positive direction, even if it feels awful;
- that I am capable of making it through any struggle.

Adversity offers a gateway for emergence on the other side as a stronger, wiser, and more compassionate person than I was before. In it I discover the sensitivity, strength and compassion that only one who has walked through the fire possesses.

Sometimes, when the world feels so chaotic, it's important for me to remember that everyone has had challenges and that spiritually we all share the same divine Light. I sense it when I'm in the presence of one who has overcome illness, addiction, loss, financial devastation, or any other natural or man-made disaster. Would any of us have asked for those circumstances? No. Would we have ever believed that we had the endurance, the will, or the courage to overcome them? No. And yet here we are with an awareness of a deep sense of our inner truth, born out of adversity.

Always at choice, I can either add to the chaos, screaming at what's wrong, or I can shine the light of my love and caring. As I let my light shine, I begin to see the light in others behind the outward appearance of their behavior, reminding me of our connection. As I let go of any feelings of separation, my optimism grows. There's a shift in consciousness happening as more and more of us shine our lights. We become beacons to others to do the same. Underneath the chaos, I believe that healing is happening.

Most importantly, I'm aware that the One that adores me is right smack in the middle of every single challenge, holding me as I move through it, guiding me to the other side. When I choose to focus on that great Love my attitude fills with the expansiveness of possibility. Sometimes solutions seem to appear out of nowhere! Sometimes they take a lot longer, but I know they're on their way. My job is to remember how resilient, capable, courageous and wise I am, stay open to the solution, let go of what it needs to look like, put one foot in front of the other and move forward with as much grace as I can muster.

Adversity connects me to everyone and everything around me, because in my struggles I realize that we've all had pain, we've all been afraid, we all want to be loved. Adversity is part of the human experience, challenges from which we learn that we are much more capable than we may have believed ourselves to be. It is the light that shines within each of us, filling us with its extraordinary love, that reminds us of how cherished we are.

~

Today I see my challenges in a new light. They are part of my human experience and I'm capable of moving through them well.

Accepting Each Situation as It Is

Recently I heard a caller on a radio station who said, "When I was nineteen I was living on the streets with my newborn son. There was a place I could go to get free formula for him. An elderly woman who volunteered there gave me a hug every time she saw me. She sometimes brought in an outfit for my baby. She never told me I shouldn't be living on the streets with a newborn. Instead she just accepted me." The woman's unconditional acceptance made a huge impact on the young mother. The older woman didn't spend time looking at what was wrong with her; instead she accepted her.

Every day I have moments which invite acceptance of *what is*. Some are small irritations and others catch my attention in bigger ways. I may find that someone has dented my car, the store is out of the product I wanted, I gained two pounds in one day, a loved one has fallen back into their old self-destructive behaviors, or I get a doctor's diagnosis that frightens me.

Whatever has happened is *what is*. Acceptance means that for now, this is the situation before me. I may not have wanted it, but here it is anyway. I'm at choice—I can make the situation wrong and become a victim, "I am upset because . . . ", or I can know that this is somehow *for* me and not against me. I ask, "How can I have this be an opportunity for growth and move through it well?" or "How can I like myself as I move through this situation?"

When I argue with reality, peace only becomes available if external circumstances change. My judgment of the situation boxes me into negativity. Choosing a state of acceptance allows me to be guided by the wisdom of my soul. Doing my best to stay in acceptance allows my subsequent shift in consciousness to create a void which invites the unlimited possibilities of the universe to be made known. Because I'm paying attention, I'm guided to next steps. Acceptance of what is becomes an avenue to greater faith, and I see the results of that trust multiplied abundantly.

If I want my life to change, today's a good day to start. I will mentally respond to one thing I hear or read with a positive outlook instead of negativity. I'll physically reply with optimism to at least one conversation, either in person, on the phone, by email or text. If I want my life to change, each day I will actively begin to participate in making the changes.

Embracing a life of happiness and unconditional acceptance, I learn to see every situation as a precious gift, brought to me by a gracious universe in order to practice being who I want to be.

～

I accept every situation as it is—for now, it's the situation before me. I choose to move through it with grace.

The Power of Personal Will

There's a lot to be said about personal will. How many of us have used will power to let go of an addiction, an unhealthy relationship or the need to have the last word? How many times has personal will helped us complete a project, stick to a new eating or exercise plan, begin a brand new adventure or say yes to self-care? Going to the dentist isn't my favorite thing, but afterward I'm glad I went. The same is true for balancing my checkbook and getting my car serviced. Will power helped me do the thing I needed to do, and the result feels good!

My Al-Anon sponsor told me to journal daily. My life was a mess, so I willed myself to get up early to do it. I journaled very early every morning, before anyone else in the house stirred. I'd start writing, letting out frustrations, asking questions, sharing my fears on paper. After about a month something changed—toward the end of my journaling time my frustrations and fears would ease up and my questions would begin to be answered through my own written words. There was a growing sense that things would be okay. My willingness to steadfastly follow my sponsor's directions to journal opened me up to my own inner wisdom, a whole new aspect of myself that I'd never known before!

Sure, my personal will sometimes runs amok and causes all kinds of chaos, but it also shows me how strong, resilient and courageous I am! My personal will was given to me by a loving Creator so that I could learn to have faith in myself.

~

*My personal will was given to me by a loving Creator so
I can learn to have faith in myself.*

Misery Loves Company

When things start to go wrong, they generally come in waves. Maybe I overslept and am running late to work, then I hit every red light and get caught behind the slowest driver in the world with no way to get around him/her. Finally I arrive at work and my boss wonders why I'm late. I feel trapped—do I tell the truth or say I had a flat tire? All day long I just can't seem to get back on an even keel—a co-worker makes a comment that sounds judgmental, triggering the insecurities that live just under the surface of my mind. I receive an email that's up for interpretation, but I see it as a personal attack. At noon I realize I don't have time to go for lunch *and* complete the work expected of me. Of course, the lunch I meant to bring is still sitting in the refrigerator!

One thought runs throughout my day: Why me? Why am I having this miserable day?

You may have heard the saying, *Misery loves company*. It applies here. Misery will find a miserable person because it loves company! The common denominator is me. When I think of my life as a garden I ask, what seeds am I planting? If I'm planting seeds of misery, I'll grow/manifest people and experiences that want to share their misery with me. We're on the same vibrational frequency called "miserable."

With each new miserable experience, my negative victim thoughts are validated, "I can't win. I am miserable because _____." The blank is generally filled in with the name of someone who has done me wrong or a challenging situation over which I feel I have no control. My thoughts often accompany an underlying feeling of "I'm doing something wrong" or "I'm not good enough." It's a cycle that repeats itself over and over as I co-create my own reality by the power of my own creative thinking. The good news is that once I plant a new seed and nurture that seed with my fresh, new positive attitude, the results will reflect that change.

Where do I find that new seed, that seed of possibility that changes misery to happiness, insecurity to confidence, fear to faith? It's right where I am, at the very center of my wonderful, magnificent being! I access it by paying attention to my own divine wisdom/ intuition/gut feeling/the God of my understanding. I become willing to listen and then take action. My life will change because I change, one new seed at a time!

~

I plant the seed of "I am worthy of a beautiful life" because it's true!

Learning to Tolerate Frustration

My vision for the world is for everyone to know how Loved they are by the God of their understanding, and that they matter in the world, just as they are. Bringing my vision to life propels me forward. It also takes me down paths that involve learning brand new skills in order to take it to the next level. With all that learning taking place frustration can set in. To stay the course I've needed to develop the capacity to tolerate frustration.

When I began to write spiritual classes it was fun because I had learned how to write curriculum as an elementary school teacher—I was in my creative comfort zone. Then, as minister of my own spiritual center, I received the divine direction to create online, self-paced classes, which was very unfamiliar territory. It threw me into a brand new realm of recording, sound waves, editing—a process much like learning a foreign language. More than once I wanted to quit. Then a gentle question would surface from deep within me that would ask, "What's working well here?" It reminded me that after much hit-and-miss practice, I'd already gotten pretty good at some of the processes. Ah, I'd forgotten to pat myself on the back for what I'd already accomplished! It was time to give myself credit, take a deep breath and keep going. There was a flow to noticing my frustration, taking a step back to realize how far I'd already come, consciously feeling good about my accomplishments, taking a deep breath and starting again. In the end I created a dozen online classes and I learned a lot about my ability to tolerate frustration in the process.

When the Beloved led me to Facebook and gently dumped me there, it was another brand new world of which I knew nothing. Whereas most of the people I knew had been on Facebook for years, I had resisted it as chatty social media. The Beloved had other ideas—Facebook was to be my new, expanded ministry, another way to bring my vision to fruition. First I needed to learn how to navigate my way through the Facebook experience. Again the frustration of being absolutely clueless was in my face, but this time I remembered to ask, "What's working well here?" Giving myself credit for each tiny learned accomplishment, I could feel my frustration lessen. When it started to build up again I'd take a deep breath or take a break, knowing that eventually I'd learn what I needed to know in order to bring my vision forward. Facebook has become a joy, as spiritual seekers from all over the world respond to my Facebook postings, just as if we were all sitting in a spiritual class together! Thank you, God.

Saying yes to your vision is most certainly going to ask you to move past what you already know into the realm of the unfamiliar, waiting to be learned. Because we're having a very human experience, frustration is liable to surface. You will learn to tolerate it and move past it because your passion will keep calling to you, and I have a hunch you'll say yes.

What vision/idea/dream is calling you, igniting a passion that wakes you up at night and urges you to take action? Pay attention! It's yours to do. Life has faith and trust in you. Let this vision move you through frustration to deepen your faith in yourself and bring your passion to life.

～

I say yes to the vision that urges me forward—it's mine
to do. I work through any frustration because I have faith
in the vision and faith in myself!

Healthy Boundaries are a Gift

I am the only one who knows how best to take care of me. Once I accept that I'm worthy of my own self-care, healthy boundaries help me get there. I'm always at choice as to how to respond to a situation. I have options. Healthy boundaries are born from those options. I have a right to my own mental, emotional and spiritual growth. I have a right to be peaceful and happy.

If hanging out with certain friends, acquaintances or family members isn't in my best interest, I can lovingly and clearly decline their invitations. As I set healthy boundaries I give others the dignity of being responsible for their own lives while I accept responsibility for mine. If being with a particular group of friends or family members compromises my commitment to a peaceful and happy life, I can say no. It's part of accepting responsibility for my life.

There are times when it's necessary to be with people I wouldn't choose to be involved with, such as at work or social situations. That's when I can put on my 'pleasant and polite' hat and set a boundary that helps me be cordial without being so friendly that they might mistake it as personally welcoming. If the situation is work related, I can smile and speak to them about business without joining in any discussion about our personal lives or offer my opinion about anything other than business. If it's in a social setting, I can smile and at the same time, refrain from being chatty—sometimes silence is a beneficial ally! My intuition becomes a good compass, letting me know if I'm heading in the right direction.

As I move forward on my spiritual journey, there have been those that I've cared deeply about and spent a lot of time with, but now we're in two different places. At first I used to berate myself, "That person was such a good friend! Do you think you're better than her/him now?" My own self-criticism was not part of taking care of me! With a loving nudge from the Beloved, I accept the fact that I'm just in a different place on the journey now—no better or worse. Everyone's path is perfect for them, but now as we come to a fork in the road, it's time for me to take a different direction. Whereas I don't try to change or control the other person's path, I no longer need to continue to walk beside them. In order to stay true to my journey, healthy boundaries help me stay true to my own direction.

In the process of setting boundaries, there's liable to be backlash from those on the other side of the boundary. This is normal and natural. Their reaction may be one of confusion and hurt and often shows up in the form of defensiveness, blame and criticism. Even though this is perfectly understandable, I needn't take on their anger and pain. They have every right to their feelings, and I can gently honor those feelings without caving into them. It's my job to take care of me. Their reactions can't influence my decision to take care of myself unless I allow it. When I'm up against the very conflicting emotions that can come in the middle of setting boundaries, I can set a healthy boundary with myself that says, "No matter what anyone else says or does, my job is to take care of myself. I am worthwhile and deserving of the life I choose for me."

~

I set healthy boundaries because I'm worth the gift of
taking care of me.

Positivity in My Relationships

When someone I love has reached a goal, we celebrate! When someone I love is stumbling, unable to find peace, self-esteem shattered, they become one of God's greatest gifts to me. It's my opportunity to accept them exactly as they are, without the need to fix them, allowing them the dignity of owning their life. My level of love and caring is expanded as I give up the need to control what their life should look like. As I back off I give them to God for safekeeping, and my faith grows.

When my kids were little I thought it was my job to worry about them. Now I know better! Sending the negative energy of my worried fear and anxiety toward anyone isn't at all helpful. Today I ask myself, "Are these thoughts going to help the situation?" If not, I dump them. Then I send positive, upbeat, God-filled, optimistic faith their way—much healthier for them and for me!

~

Allowing those I love the dignity of taking responsibility
for their own life is a powerful act of love.
Instead of trying to control the situation, I give them to
God for safekeeping.

The Strength of Vulnerability

After joining Al-Anon my sponsor took me to her New Thought spiritual center. Because I was still atheist, she wanted to help me get over my very snippy attitude about church and that whole God-thing. Although I had my doubts, I was determined to heal myself, so I went. Within the first few visits something shifted in me and I started to cry. Caught off guard, I realized I hadn't cried in years—I was too busy being the strong one, holding everything and everyone together. Now I found myself in a safe place where no one knew me. In the safety of this place I began to feel years of fear, hurt, guilt, anger, disappointment and sorrow, and I wept through most of each service.

For several months I cried in that church. I didn't get to know people, volunteer or take a class, instead I let myself just *be*. My tears embraced and washed away feelings that had been stuffed down so long that I didn't know they existed. By stuffing them they hadn't gone away—instead my heart had become heavy and somewhere in the process I lost who I was. I was so busy being what everyone else needed me to be that I no longer knew who I was or what I needed. Before I could find myself again, those feelings needed to surface and be felt before they could be released. In the sanctuary of that spiritual center, I felt those feelings and wept with the enormity of it.

Seeing my tears, no one passed me a tissue, asked what was wrong or told me everything would be okay. Instead they just let me cry. For that I was beyond grateful! I wanted to be left alone. Healing was taking place, which required time to run its course. In the process of my healing I came to understand that I didn't need to hold the weight of the world on my shoulders. It was okay to fall apart. I could actually let others see my pain. I could let *me* see my pain.

We all have our stuff. We're either hiding it, denying it, wallowing in it, learning from it, working through it or we're on the other side of it. No longer will I beat myself up because my life doesn't look like I think it should look. It looks exactly how it's supposed to look because it's *my* life. Sometimes I'm afraid. Sometimes I'm angry, resentful and unforgiving. It's okay to be human. It's okay to have human feelings. It's okay not to know what to do. It's okay to mess up. In my willingness to let others see the authentic me—the one who doesn't have it all together, I no longer have to pretend to be strong. I can let the authentically imperfect me be seen as I stand strong in who I am, just as I am and just as I am not. What a relief to accept my life as it is and just be myself!

~

I am strong in my vulnerability, allowing myself to show up just as I am and just as I am not.

My Gratitude is Creative

There's a quiet energy of peace around the person who lives their life in gratitude. When a troublesome situation makes its way into their lives, they immediately look for something to be grateful for. Instead of angst, there's a sense of calmness about them. Gratitude is alive and well in all of us. When I make it a priority, my life begins to change, too.

I used to move through much of my day on auto pilot, just getting things done. Now that I appreciate the sacredness of life I look for what's beautiful and see it all around me. The grooves in the bark of a tree delight my senses as I reach out to trace their path. The clouds dancing in the sky, playing hide and seek with the sun, bring a smile to my face. Life is alive with beauty if I'll take the time to notice. Noticing the small things brings me to a state of quiet appreciation. While gratitude seems so simple, it's really very powerful!

Appreciation lifts me out of despair because I can't be truly grateful and despairing at the same time. It turns me away from the problem and toward what's possible. I ask myself, "What aspect of my divine nature can I bring to this situation – peace, acceptance, love, wisdom?" The more I stay centered on the spiritual gift that's emerging within me, the quicker the problem dissolves!

The universe is alive, awake and ready to sense my message of appreciation for the simple things around me. The result? I get more for which to be grateful.

That's the way life works! My inner song of appreciation leads to acceptance of life, just as it is. No matter what's going on, if I look for the positive in myself and in my life it brings about a feeling of hope and possibility. Even if my life feels like it's turned upside down in the moment, a powerful tool is to find something—anything—to be grateful for. It takes the focus off of what's wrong and replaces it with what's right, which opens the door to solutions. The universe senses the energy of my appreciation, acts on it, and more reasons to be grateful start to show up.

Gratitude is the most natural thing in the world. It was born into all of us at the moment of creation. We can tap into it when we're praying, meditating, creating, dancing, or connecting with someone we love, including our pets. It happens in the present moment when we're awake and aware. Each moment, no matter what's happening, is an invitation to feel grateful.

∼

Knowing that my gratitude is creative, I find something to be grateful for in each situation.

Seeing the Goodness in the World

There is so much good in the world! Seeing it depends upon where I put my focus. Whereas the media tends to catch our attention with negativity, I can look at the world through eyes of positivity. Just think of all the parents or guardians who will speak lovingly to their children today or will sooth a feverish brow with a cool washcloth. How many dogs will be walked, joyfully sniffing every object in their path? How many bikes will be ridden, recycle bins filled, and trees planted? Just think of the addicts who will seek recovery today, knowing that they are ready to turn their life around. Millions will have the courage to say, "I'm sorry," or ask for help, or stand up for themselves in a challenging situation. Many will go to work today doings jobs that they love, knowing that they are making a difference in the world. Others will pray, adding their highest thoughts and intentions to the positive energy that's alive in our universe.

How many funny stories will cause a moment of joy today? Picture the homemade cakes, pies and pastries that will be served, delicious even though a bit lopsided. Then there are the employees complimented by their bosses who will go on to do an even better job because they are beaming inside. Teachers will encourage their students, and schools will acknowledge the efforts of their teachers. Volunteers in every walk of life will eagerly show up, ready to be of service, knowing that they make the world a better place. Pets will be adopted from animal shelters all over the world. Contractors and their workers will see the happiness on the faces of clients whose living space has been made new because of their time and expertise. Patients, with grateful tears in their eyes, will take the time to thank the nurses, doctors and technicians who were part of their healing. Hospice workers will forever feel the gratitude of the families of loved ones who have passed.

I visualize doors being held open by for the person behind them by strangers with smiling faces, drivers allowing the next car to merge, and people waiting patiently in lines across the world. Today there will be millions of people saying, "Thank you" to another. Imagine how many will hear "I love you" or "I'm grateful for you," in every language imaginable!

We were created from the greatest Love of all—it's our nature to be kind, considerate, and so joy-filled that it spills out to touch everyone and everything around us. It's natural to share our love. There is a reason that I'm alive in this day and time, participating in the goodness that abounds in the world. The energetic vibration of my enthusiasm, along with the enthusiasm of everyone who does their best to look on the bright side, uplifts the energy of the world. We really can make a joyful difference!

~

With gratitude, I focus on and participate in the
goodness that's alive and well in the world today.

Chapter 7

I Am a Seeker

ANYONE ON A SPIRITUAL PATH becomes a seeker of truth. As a seeker, I have a lot of questions. If left to my own devices I think the stories in my head are the truth, but I learned long ago that I've made up those stories in order to make sense about how things came to be the way they are. The stories are interesting, but they aren't the truth. The truth comes from a different Source. I've become very practiced at tuning into my heart space, that quiet place of wisdom where the Beloved responds to my many questions.

It's Okay to Ask

I can ask the Beloved anything! Even if I'm angry, defiant and challenging, Love stands ready to hear my complaints. If I'm feeling sorry for myself, it holds me in my misery until its love smooths out the wrinkles of my discontent. Because the Beloved knows me intimately, it already knows my questions, so why not ask them?

In fact, I think that sometimes the Beloved plants questions in my mind because I'm finally ready to hear the answer, knowing that the inner dialog that comes from it will stretch my understanding of how Life works.

This chapter contains some of the questions I've asked, along with the Beloved's answers. When I ask the question, the energy of the Beloved holds me close so that I can sense its presence. Sometimes the answer comes quickly and sometimes I wait hours, days, weeks or months for it. There are some questions that haven't yet been answered, or maybe they have been answered but I haven't consciously recognized the answer. No worries! When the time is right I will feel the answer coming from deep within my own heart, in thoughts, words or pictures that my mind will understand. Sometimes the answers show up in the words of another, an unexpected phone call, an inspired passage in a book, the perfect message on social media, or the personalized license plate of the car in front of me. Once I as the question, it's up to me to know I've been heard. I will stay open to the answer in whatever form it shows up.

～

When something's on my mind I can take it straight to
the God of my understanding for answers.

How Do I Sense Your Presence?

As an atheist I had denied the presence of any kind of a Higher Power. When I first realized that God was real, I somehow knew that it had always been there, loving me even when I was making fun of people who believed in God. I asked, "I spent the first fifty years of my life not believing in you, but I have a hunch you were there all along. Why couldn't I see you or sense your presence?"

The Beloved answered:

"*You're right, dearest one . . . I was there all along. I'm always there. For those first fifty years you weren't ready to know me, but I was still there, cherishing you in the middle of your celebrations and at the depths of your sorrows. As you made your own choices, I used those choices to co-create the life you were choosing to live. You didn't know this, of course, so you kept thinking that life was happening to you, when in reality life was responding to you. All the while, I was right where you were, wanting only your highest happiness. That's my greatest wish for you, you know—to be happy. Do you remember when you were a frightened child with nightmares about snakes trying to get into your bed? I was the bed that kept the snakes away. I was the covers you hid under. I was the pillow that you buried your head in. I was the courage you found to get through the night. I was the morning realization that everything was okay.*

Do you remember those many times as a teenager when you rebelled, going against everything you knew was "right" to purposefully do what was "wrong"? Inside you were a jumble of excitement, fear, and guilt, jumping into situations that put you at risk physically and emotionally. I was there as your intuition, keeping you from doing something from which you couldn't recover. I was there as divine guidance, helping you to learn from each experience as you discovered that you were much more than you thought yourself to be. I was the thought in your head that said, "Say no," or "Leave right now," when danger was imminent. Because you were in your very human rebellious stage, sometimes you paid attention and sometimes you didn't. I was there when it worked out and when you ended up in a heap of trouble. I held your hand when you realized you had gone too far. I comforted you as you sobbed from being hurt. I gave you the courage to begin the next day. Because you have free will, you lived with the results of your choices. How else will you learn the effects of your choices unless you dive in to live them? Whether the results were positive or negative, to me you were nothing short of wonderful! Always, I loved you without reservation, even when you didn't like yourself very much.

Think back to all the times in your life that were really hard. I walked you through them. You leaned on me when you cried so hard you thought you'd never stop. I gave you the strength to take the next step when you wanted to quit. I held you close when you did quit, giving up on yourself and the world. Then I gave you the willingness to dig down deep within yourself to start again . . . to keep going. It worked! You're still here, aren't you? Somehow, you believed in yourself enough to persevere, and I was there.

By the time you reached age fifty you were drained by the choices you had made, and that's when you opened the door to know me. Do you remember that day in your living room, shortly after your 50th birthday, when you asked, "Is this it? Is this all my life is about?" The first thought you had was, "I need to go back to Al-Anon." That was me! In the past you wouldn't have noticed that thought, let alone taken it seriously, but now you were ready. You were worn out enough from doing life your own way, the best you knew how, and now you were open to new possibilities. You were getting ready to know yourself as a spiritual being. You were getting ready to know me. Together, you and I were preparing to create a new life because *you* had changed. You were already choosing a new path.

I want you to know that within you is everything you need to live the life that you want to live. I live in you, as you. You could never be separate from me. Whatever path you choose to take, I'm right there, taking it with you. Because I love you I'm always planting seeds of my love into your mind. Sometimes you sense them and sometimes you don't. Both are okay—it's your free will. The one thing I want you to know is that I'll never stop being with you. My love is unconditional. I love you, plain and simple."

~

Wherever I am, whatever I'm doing, I am cherished by a God that adores me that's right there with me.

What Makes an Awakening Real?

Many times I asked the Beloved One, "Why is it that my first experience of you was so powerful that I couldn't turn away from it? In that moment, when I least expected it, I awakened to your Presence. Everything changed because of that one experience! Somehow I knew for sure that you were real and that you loved me unconditionally. How does that happen? What did you do? What did I do?" It took a long time (I've learned to be very patient) but finally the Beloved answered:

"*Good questions!* Awakening to my presence as Divine Love is certainly a life-changing experience. People awaken in many different ways, anything from a sudden feeling of being connected to everything as they watch the sun rise to feeling my unconditional Love when they've hit an emotional or spiritual bottom.

Once a person awakens to my presence they have a choice—shake it off and go on with their lives as usual *or know it's true and allow their lives to change. It's a big decision, one that's usually made in a split second. Many view the experience as an once-in-a-lifetime occurrence, tucking it away in their memory while giving it no relevance in the practicality of their life today. It's often seen as coincidence or an unusual, unexplainable happening as the mind tries to make logical sense of it. Sometimes potential awakening experiences are chalked up to happenstance, "Wow, how amazing was that?!" and then they are released as the person gets on with the life they're used to—the phone call from a friend, bills to be paid or wondering what to have for dinner, as the moment recedes to the back of their mind.*

Every time a person chooses the busyness of human life, the awakening slips away. No problem! I'm infinitely patient. I want my creation to know me, so I continually offer indications that I'm right there—the answer to a question, the solution to an ongoing problem, the perfect words to say when you're feeling inadequate, the vitality from a good night's sleep, the beauty of nature, the sudden feeling that everything is going to be okay. That's me! My love is eternal and my devotion ongoing. As each person goes through their everyday life, I will continue to find a way to invite them to awaken to my presence.

A personal awakening takes place when the choice is made to believe that the amazing, unexplained experience they had was real. A conscious decision is made to focus on it, and thus begins a personal relationship with me. The person moves past God as a good idea to having a personal experience with me, now the God of their understanding.

As you've discovered, knowing me changes your life. Once you notice and pay attention to the Love that dwells within you and all around you, you can't un-know it. That's what happened with you. Because you chose to focus on me, you came to understand that life continuously presents you with demonstrations of my Love, simply because you exist. Sunrise is not just a strikingly spectacular time of the day, it is your personal gift, a direct experience of my Love, "I give this to you as a reflection of the beauty I see in you." Your next great idea is brought to you by your own inner wisdom, quietly directing you toward your fullest potential. Awakening is an invitation to see that everything in your life comes from a gracious universe that overflows with abundance.

Awakening happens all at once for some, like it did with you, but usually it's a process. Because change and letting go are important parts of living a spiritual life, it can look and feel like chaos. It's kind of like taking a snapshot photo of a chick making its way out of the shell — it's a struggle and the chick looks overwhelmed. Once you see the result, you realize the process was necessary. Developing a personal relationship with me is much the same thing. You take risks that you would never have dared before because now you know you aren't alone. In the darkest times I find a way to remind you of the light — you find hope through a song's message or a phrase in the book you're reading; the perfect words or images show up on your computer screen; you feel unexplained joy from watching the antics of a pet. Highly aware that I am in all things, all the time, you feel my presence holding the light for you until you can see it for yourself. More and more, as your faith grows, you become the light for others and for yourself. You shine the truth of who you are because you are no longer hiding it. As you awaken to the fullness of the beauty of who you are, others will notice, and eventually they'll realize that the same light shines within them.

~

> *Know that I am at the center of every situation as pure Love. Look for me and you'll find me. Awaken and you will know me. "*

Now I realize that the peace I felt that night in 1998 was just God doing what God does constantly, with all of us. The only difference is that while I was in the moment, I focused on it! For the first time in my life I had surrendered my intellect's need for logical explanations and paid attention to the extraordinary peaceful stillness that I was feeling. I finally understood that the only reason I had such a huge experience of God, one that changed my life forever, is because I paid attention! It was no greater or less than that. The Beloved hadn't changed — I had changed!

The same can be true for you. The God of your understanding is seeking your attention in this moment. Are you willing to believe it? Are you willing to know how Loved you are? Are you willing to believe you are treasured, even if your life is an absolute mess? If you aren't sure, just say yes, pretend that the God of your understanding is real and is right where you are in this moment. Then sit in silence to see what thoughts and feelings come up. You truly aren't alone.

If you have already had a personal awakening, what did it look and feel like? What were the circumstances? What emotions were present? How has the awakening changed your life? The more you focus on what's true for you about the God of your understanding, the more you invite Divine Love into your life. No matter where we are on the spiritual path, we are all mightily blessed!

~

> *In every situation . . . at all times . . . Divine Love is seeking my attention so that I can know how Loved I am.*

How Do I Learn to Have Faith in Myself?

I challenged the Beloved, "You tell me that I'm wonderful, exactly as I am, even when my life is turned upside down. You tell me that you love me unconditionally, just because I exist. You say that I'm a gift to the world and that I came here, to this time and place, to *be* the gift that I am. With all the faith and trust you have in me, why don't I have that kind of faith and trust in myself?"
The Beloved answered:

"*You were brought to this life experience to give the gift of yourself to the world. You give your gift by being gloriously happy, engaging in activities that cause you to feel alive inside! The energy of your happiness can be felt throughout the world, and it's contagious! Others will feel better simply because you are doing what makes you happy. Therefore, your happiness uplifts the world!*

You have everything you need to live a life that's alive, joyous and free. The moment I created you I planted the seeds of wisdom, courage, clarity and creativity within you, as well as every other aspect of spiritual truth that can act as tools to bring you to your highest happiness. You have courage you haven't even tapped into yet. You've had a sense of it. Think back to a time you were so terrified that you didn't think you could possibly make it. Then somehow you got through it. How do you think you did that? You have within you the ability to be courageous because you are courage.

Even though you see yourself as very average intellectually, you are wiser than you believe yourself to be. Consider situations in which it was important to make a wise decision, and somehow you chose one that was helpful. You have within you the ability to make wise decisions because *you are wisdom.*

Relationships can teach you a lot about yourself. Just think about all those tricky relationship challenges that caused you to doubt yourself. Scratching your head and wondering what to do next, you intuitively made a choice that turned out well. Recall the times when you needed to find the right words to say to someone who was hurting and you thought, "What words can I possibly say that will be helpful?" And then, from someplace deep inside you, you found them. Just the right words came out of your mouth to be supportive and caring. You have within you the ability to know what to do and say because *you are intuition and compassion.*

The human experience is filled with challenges that have shaken you to your core by circumstances you didn't expect and didn't want. Those situations are opportunities from which to grow the self-respect and self-compassion that dignifies the confusion, disappointment and pain you felt, turning those difficult times into insightful teachers. When you look back with a gentle open heart, you just may realize that you deserve your own self-care and self-love because *you are love.*

You are my gift to the world, exactly as you are. You will learn to have faith and trust in yourself when you begin to see you through my eyes . . . the eyes of truth. You are my beloved one. You are the world's beloved one. Accept it. Live it. Know that you matter in the world. "

～

I am made of the same stuff as the One that created me, here to give the gift of ME to the world.

Why Do I Play Small?

I've had opportunities to shine, and yet I've held back. It's almost embarrassing to put myself out there. So many doors to success have presented themselves "Choose me! Open me!" yet, the unknown made me hesitate to open them, let alone walk through them. I asked the Beloved, "Why do I often have a tendency to play small? Is it really okay to put myself first?" The Beloved answered:

"It is true that you are meant to shine! In every situation, your job is to ask yourself, "What do I need in order to shine my light in this circumstance?" and then follow the inner guidance you are given. It takes courage, and you have that courage. It takes a feeling of self-worth, and you are learning that you are worthy. It also takes a willingness to let go of old beliefs that may be telling you to play small. This may take a good deal of practice because up to this point, you have been programmed not to call attention to yourself . . . to put others first . . . to dim your ability to shine.

As a child you may have been taught not to stand out, to give your opinion or say what you need. You were warned that anything else was self-centered or selfish. Of course, those well-meaning people were only telling you what they had been taught. Remember, everyone is doing the best they can with the consciousness they have at the time.

Today's a new day! You are meant to shine in every situation! You'll know how to stand up, give your opinion and say what you need with grace and poise. There's a time and place to put others first, but it doesn't mean you should play small. When you're standing in your own light, you have an unlimited ability to put others first because you know who you are. You'll know what to say and do, how to say and do it, and when to respectfully remain quiet. As you let your light shine, you're giving from the overflow of your own peace, your own joy, your own love. Putting yourself first means being centered in who you truly are and then coming from that space as you give your gift.

It's also important to put yourself first because now you believe that you're good enough to do so. Your choices are creative. Every time you play small, your feeling of self-worth diminishes. The universe pays attention to how you feel. The universe senses, "I'm not good enough," and because it acts on your thoughts without judging them, you will get more reasons to not to feel good enough. Your lack of self-worth tends to affect many areas of your life, and you often end up with less money, fewer happy relationships, or declining health because there's an internal message that says you don't deserve it.

For instance, if you want more money and have prayed for prosperity and then you find a dime, you're at creative choice. You can be dissatisfied because it's only a dime or be thrilled because it's evidence of answered prayer. The universe is listening, paying attention to where you put your emotional energy: Money = Disappointment or Money = Joy. When you play small you tend to feel disappointment, so you get more to feel disappointed about.

Because my will for you is to be happy, start putting yourself first. Find a reason to shine simply because you are worthy of shining! Consciously build your relationship with yourself. Know that you live in a universe that's on your side, creating from the vibration of your emotional energy. Tap into your courage . . . the courage to let go of what's not serving you and to say yes to what excites you. Let go of old beliefs that tell you you're being selfish. Pay attention to what makes you happy and do more of that. The light you shine from the energy of your inner joy enriches the world!"

~

As I say yes to me, I shine a light that enriches the world.

Why is the Human Race So Messed Up?

Our human lives seem so chaotic. We all want to be loved. We all want to be happy. We all want inner peace, don't we? And yet humans seem to create a never-ending amount of suffering for ourselves and for each other. I asked, "Why is the human race is so messed up?"

The Beloved answered:

"*When I created all that there is, I did so with great, loving confidence. Within that confidence I gave you free will—the ability to think for yourself and then make choices from those thoughts. The universe is a great creative mechanism and responds automatically to your choices. What you think about . . . dwell upon . . . worry about . . . get excited about . . . is creative. As the universe, I co-create your life with you depending upon what you are thinking. Your life becomes a mirror of what's going on within you. If you're mostly happy, your life will be mostly happy. If you're mostly unhappy, your life will be mostly unhappy. I don't judge your happiness or unhappiness—I just respond to it. That's how free will works.*

Free will offers you an invitation. If your life isn't going the way you want it to go, you can adopt new thoughts.

The person who can turn everything around is you! I have confidence that you will do what is right for you, and the only one who knows what that looks like is you. No matter what your choice is, or what path your life takes because of the choices you've made, I love you completely and forever, just as you are. Nothing you think, say or do will stop that.

Each person in the human race is making choices. To me, none of you are messed up. Each person is simply living their free will. I hold everyone and everything with love as they go about living the life they are choosing for themselves. If their life is miserable, they are paying a lot of attention to negative thoughts, which invites more misery into their lives. They can turn this around by changing the way they respond to their circumstances. When the negative energy of their thoughts becomes more positive, their circumstances will begin to change. That's the way it works. The concept is simple to understand. Practicing it in everyday life is what the human experience is all about.

What you put into your life you will get out of it. Once you become aware that the direction of your life is up to you, you can choose to keep taking that same path or choose a new one. That's free will. It really is all about you, my beloved one."

~

With my free will I make choices that head my life in a positive direction.

How Do I Get Past My Fears?

I was at the end of my 30-year marriage when I discovered that God was real. I had been married since I was twenty-one, and at age 51

I didn't even know how to live life as a single person! Even though I knew I had to leave, I was terrified of floundering in a world that was outside the familiar activities of married life. My question was, "How do I get past my fear?" The Beloved answered:

"It's okay to be afraid. It's part of the human experience. You were afraid lots of times in your marriage, too, and you made it through each of those challenges. Think back to some of them now. When your husband or one of your kids was sick or in trouble, you didn't let your fear stop you because your intention was to find a way to help. In times of financial crisis your fear acted as a catalyst to become financially more aware, a trait that still guides your life. When you ventured past being a stay-at-home mom in order to go back to college, your fear of the unknown didn't stop you—instead you worked through it to take charge of your own dreams . . . your own happiness. You did everything necessary to become a teacher, which had always been your dream!

Your fear has caused drama in your life, and you've learned and grown from that, too. Once you discovered that I was real, a new passion was born—you wanted the whole world to know how Loved they are and that they matter, just as they are. You wanted to shout it from the rooftops! Do you remember how terrified you used to be to speak in front of others? You jumped over many fear-based hurdles to get to the point where you could do it.

Being in front of others means wearing your vulnerability on your sleeve. Do you remember that time in third grade when you were asked to be a participant in the talent show? A friend was going to sing a song to you, and all you needed to do was sit there? You were so afraid to be on the stage in front of everyone that you said no. It was much safer to blend in with the audience. Then later you thought, "I could have done that!" and you tucked that awareness into your memory bank.

Of course you recall the fourth grade incident when, after giving your first oral report, you returned to your desk and involuntarily emptied your bladder, unable to stop even as the entire class looked on in shock. The humiliation was deep and long lasting. You wanted your parents to move, or at least let you attend another school, but of course that didn't happen. You returned, dealt with the humiliation, and one day at a time, got on with your life. From that experience a seed of compassion was planted for others in embarrassing situations.

In high school you had to take public speaking as a college requirement. Terrified of further shame, you didn't drink anything before the designated class so that there would be nothing in your bladder, that fourth grade incident never far from your mind. You memorized your speeches because you were afraid of making a public mistake. It was gut wrenchingly difficult, but you did it.

In college, on your way to becoming a teacher, another public speaking class was necessary. By this time you discovered that you could waver from memorization because you were finally becoming more comfortable in front of others. Slowly, slowly, slowly you were learning to trust yourself.

Finally, your kids half grown, you jumped into your dream of being an elementary school teacher! You learned to have fun in front of a classroom full of children! When back-to-school night came around, you had just as good a time with their parents. You believed in yourself as a teacher, and you had gotten on the other side of your fear of being in front of others to live the dream that brought *you so much happiness.*

Because you didn't let your fears stop you, you discovered that being in front of others could feel fulfilling and joyous. You had no idea that every challenge had been pivotal in bringing your message about me to the world. Now you are a minister, a speaker and a writer, rejoicing in speaking in front of others who are on a spiritual path!

There is a gift in every single experience. Life often throws people into the fire, and courage walks them out of it. Thank you for saying yes to your courage and to your life."

~

One step at a time I move through my fears, knowing that there is a gift in every life experience.

What Do I Do with Everyday Stress?

Our human lives seem to be loaded with stress, which definitely isn't conducive to happiness. I decided to bring my concerns to the Beloved, "It seems like stress is part of everyday living. People go to jobs they don't like, with work situations that are stressful. Families struggle with all kinds of relationship issues. Almost everyone has financial stress. More and more, addictions take over our lives. Health issues arise from all that stress, and the health issues exacerbate the stress. There must be something we can do!" The Beloved answered:

"Do you remember when you were a child, awakening to the sunshine making its way through your window, inviting you to join the day? Flying out of bed, barely taking time to eat, you could hardly wait to see what life had to offer! There were balls to kick,

games to play and fireflies to catch in a jar. There were silly
made-up jokes shared with friends, roaring with laughter
at how witty you were! Do you recall those solitary
moments lying on the grass, staring at the summer clouds
in the vast blue expanse overhead? You became a sculptor
carving out creation in the shapes that materialized in
the white fluffy stuff. Entering into personal dialog with
yourself, you marveled at what appeared, "Look, there's a
bear! Its head is on the left and its body down lower, to the
right. I can even make out its tail!" You watched the bear
shift with the breeze until it finally disappeared to leave
you searching for your next great discovery. Shaking the
grass out of your clothes as you finally stood up to leave,
you delighted in your own creative brilliance, there for the
taking amidst the tapestry of nature's bounty.

Reflecting upon those memories, can you feel your body
relaxing, the urge to grin twitching at the corners of your
mouth? Good! Welcome back to my world, a world where
the simplicity of life connects you with the uncomplicated,
down-to-earth treasures found in the beauty, potential and
happiness inherent in life itself. It's the life you're meant to
live. I'm on a great adventure as you, forever seeking your
attention so that you might awaken to the joy and glory of
what's in front of you and the magnificence of who you
are in it.

You may be thinking, "That was a long time ago,
and there's a lot of difference between then and now!"
Really, there is less than you realize. Sure, you have
work to accomplish, bills to pay, families to support and
appointments to keep. Your days are very full! With that
in mind, ask yourself some questions: Just how are my
days being filled? Do I see life as a great adventure? Did
I notice the clouds, the trees or any other aspect of nature

today? Do I take time for quiet reflection every day? Have I laughed out loud lately? Have I paid attention to what makes me happy? Do I even know what makes me happy?

Living fully is not meant to be complicated. It's possible to experience daily the deliciousness that life has to offer. Pretend that each day is a lifetime. When you go to bed at night, do you feel fulfilled as you reflect upon the last twenty-four hours? The answers may help you understand what is most important to you. Is it your new stylish furniture or the contentment you feel as you walk through the door of your home at night? Will your new job promotion be at the top of your list, or your relationships with your co-workers? Is it important that you accomplished the things that made others happy, or what made you happy? Life is a balance. When your own happiness becomes a priority, you'll take the measures needed to engage in activities that you enjoy so much that stress falls away, replaced with the joy of being alive.

You get to choose where to put your attention. You get to decide to set aside time every day to just *be*. Remember that you have the free will to make your own choices, and the universe is paying attention to what you choose. If you choose stressful situations, the universe thinks that's what's important to you so you'll get more of them. If you choose to make time for life's simple enjoyments, the universe will give you more enjoyable opportunities. You really are a co-creator, holding the key to your own happiness. Only you can decide to open the door."

~

I choose to open the door to happiness, making time for simple enjoyments

Chapter 8

I Am Willing

I AM WILLING TO CHANGE . . . to let go of anger, fear, judgment and needless suffering, so I turn to prayer. I pray for lots of reasons, and my prayer takes many forms. As an atheist I had no idea how to pray, and happily I discovered that the "how" wasn't important!

Prayer Changes Me

I first explored a rudimentary form of prayer at the end of my marriage, shortly after I knew God was real. I was such a confused, frightened mess that I didn't know which end was up. I'd go into the bathroom, the only room in the house with a lock, lie on the floor and cry. Coming up from the depths of despair I'd whisper, "Help me." Somehow I knew I was heard. Within a few minutes to a few hours, I'd get what I needed, even though I wasn't at all sure what it was that I needed. But the Beloved knew. If I needed strength or courage it would well up within me and I'd know what to do with it. If I needed to set a boundary I'd know when and how to do it. If I needed to take a time-out and just be alone, that's what I'd do. I prayed that simple prayer over and over, each time my faith deepening as I came to understand that the Beloved knew what I needed long before me. Before my prayer was uttered, it was heard.

As my relationship with the Divine deepened, I experimented with prayer, exploring what worked best for me. There was a time when I struggled with negativity toward someone, so I folded them into my prayers. I tucked them in between the people I loved most dearly and wished them the same goodness that I wished for my loved ones. At first it was hard, but as time went on it got easier. The result? God's grace took over. Negativity was gone. My prayers were answered. I realized that prayer changes the one praying, and that's me.

When something happens in the world that catches my attention and fills me with angst, I remember that the power of Divine Love is fully present in all places, at all times, for all beings. That same Divine Love is within me. In the quiet of my own home I lean into Love. I feel its power, and in prayer I send the energy of that Love to the situation that needs it. The optimistic energy of my prayer is the most positive and powerful gift I can offer.

If I'm tempted to fret about someone I love, I know that sending them my worried energy isn't at all helpful. The Beloved offers an alternative. "Give her/him to me. I will hold her. I will tend to him. I'm doing it now." Like a priceless gift, I give them to the greatest Love of all. I picture the energy of love—like soft mist—surrounding and filling them, holding them close. The Beloved offers as much healing and joy as my loved one will allow. It finds ways to show them that they aren't alone. As I release them to the Beloved I find peace, and my peaceful energy *is* helpful—it sends a message of faith and hope.

The greatest comfort I've ever known is when I give everything over to the Beloved and collapse, exhausted, into its grace. There I am, with all my judgments (including self-judgment), fear, hurt and self-doubt, beating myself up for feeling consumed by negativity. Then the Beloved beckons, "I'm here. I'll take care of you. I know you're doing the best you can. Let me hold you." Just as the Beloved holds the world, it holds me.

Prayer reminds me that there's a part of me that only knows love. I pray to always see through the eyes of that great love, letting the goodness of God within me guide my thoughts, my words and my actions. Even though I live in an imperfect body, in an imperfect world, I can choose to see it rightly when I hold each situation in the perfection of the greatest Love of all.

~

I pray for many reasons, knowing my prayers are always heard. The beauty of prayer is that it changes the one praying, and that's me.

Listening to My Intuition

When I'm at odds with another over how something should be handled, it's an opportunity to learn from the deepest part of me. Instead of my knee-jerk, "My way is the right way" reaction, I can open myself up to a greater understanding, one that doesn't include my need to control the situation. If I can stop long enough to take a deep breath, I create a pathway to the innate, wise, instinctive part of me—my intuition. If I'm willing to pull back for a moment and really listen to the other person's point of view, I give my intuition a chance to hear it.

I am so much more than my own thoughts, which are mostly stories I've made up from past experiences. My intuition is a gateway between who I am as a spiritual being and who I am in my human experience. It teams up with my body (as a gut reaction) to lead me to the very best response in any particular situation.

My intuition is a link to my soul . . . my spiritual essence. It offers me an immediate understanding of what to do without the need for my very human mind to try to figure it out. There's a greater truth in each situation, one that I can't always see. I often feel my intuition as an amazing new idea that comes out of 'nowhere,' without any logical reasoning. I sometimes feel it as a gut reaction that tells me if I'm heading in the right direction. I know when I'm following my intuition and when I'm not, as one feels empowering and the other feels like I'm walking through slush. My intuition helps my mind connect with the gut feeling in my body, and I suddenly have a sense as to what to do next.

Today I'm better at trusting my intuition in everyday situations. If I'm in a circumstance that I intuitively know isn't right for me, I can walk away from it. When I feel fear about moving toward a dream that I intuitively know is right for me, I know I can feel the fear without letting it stop me. My part is to give my intuition a chance . . . to listen to it and act on it. If I keep thinking I have the only right answer, I close the door on my intuition.

It's humbling to step back and wait for a greater understanding. Each time I say yes to my intuition, my faith grows as I discover a world that's greater than what goes on in my own head. There's much more to me than I ever imagined! In every way I am set up to succeed.

~

As I tune into and act on the wisdom of my intuition, I'm guided toward success.

Surrender Equals Safety

In my everyday life I learn to be discerning, saying yes when appropriate and no when necessary. I set boundaries with the people around me, "Not now, thank you," and with myself, "You know if you eat that cookie you'll only want another one!" A bit of caution is important in my human experience. However, the spiritual realm is an entirely different matter! Following my inner wisdom is always the right choice, even when I don't understand its call. When I am in tune with who I really am, I instinctively say yes. The more I follow the Beloved's gentle urgings, the happier and freer I am. Building my life on faith and trust, my world opens up to possibilities I never knew existed!

Surrender is a word that often carries a negative connotation, as visions of a white flag signify that someone has lost the battle. The question becomes, if I surrender to the God of my understanding, what am I losing: the need to be right, the demand that my expectations be met, jumping to conclusions, taking things personally, or feeling jealous when I witness another's success?

The ability to live my life fully without the need to control the world is my invitation to freedom. Surrender means letting go of manipulation. Instead I open up to the power of Love within me, "I am here, as you. You already have the answers. Your greatest happiness exists now, in this moment, if you are willing to let it emerge." I'm guided to next steps instead of trying to force them. The experience of developing a personal relationship with God has become my ticket to an empowering, joyous life, with freedom as my reward. The more I surrender, the more I am liberated from the negativity that festers like a sore waiting to be healed.

My devotion to the God of my understanding comes from personal experience. As an atheist, I wasn't taught about God, so when I discovered God was real the relationship was personal to *me*, which was a perfect set-up for surrender. In that first moment of awakening, I felt divine peace and love. The Beloved knew me intimately and adored me, just as I was, with all the messiness of my life, which was pretty messy at the time! Why wouldn't I surrender to that great Love? Why shouldn't I follow its lead? After all, I wasn't doing so well on my own.

I quickly learned that the Beloved was trustworthy. I experimented with it, trying to figure out where I stood with this Presence that I couldn't see but instinctively knew was the most important part of my life. I'd choose a situation, anything from setting a boundary to deciding what to cook for dinner. "Here, I give this to you. Tell me what to do and I'll do it. Guide me through it—I'm paying attention. I give the outcome to you." It worked every time! Not only did I come away liking myself in the situation, but with every experiment, I learned that the One that guided me wanted the best outcome for everyone. It expanded my compassion and loosened the grip of my need for control. It was safe to trust. It was safe to surrender to Love.

When I'm tempted to be less than okay with the way things are and the urge to control rises to the surface, the Beloved One scoops me up. It holds me close to remind me of how cherished I am, that life is on my side, that everything will be okay. "Breathe faith in and let me carry you through this." Reminded of what's true, I let go and allow myself to be carried. That's surrender.

In every situation there's a bigger picture than what I can see. Fully present in the moment (especially when it's hard) I turn toward the One that wants the highest and best for all of us. My perspective shifts. I listen for divine direction, and then I act on it. There's no need to understand the big picture—my only job is to trust that it's there. I'm safe in Love's care.

~

No matter the external circumstances, I'm safe in the loving care of a God that adores me. I surrender to that great Love and know that I am safe.

The Choice to Forgive

The opportunity to forgive is a critical part of my ongoing journey as a spiritual being having a human experience. Every time someone takes my parking space or cuts me off on the freeway, there's the opportunity! When I get passed over for a raise at work, my perpetually tardy friend is thirty minutes late, or the neighbor's dog is barking, there it is again! It's in irritating everyday events as well as the big, hurtful occurrences that turn my world upside down. What I do with each situation is up to me. Forgiveness is an option that only I can choose; it's an inside job.

Anything that disturbs my peace is cause for forgiveness. I may ask, "Why should I be the one to forgive? I didn't do anything! I'm the one who was hurt! If I forgive the other person, am I condoning what they did? Isn't forgiveness sending them the message that what they did was okay? Sometimes I think my resentments keep me safe—if I forgive am I opening myself up to be hurt again? Yes, I want to be healed. Yes, I want to be peaceful.

How do I get past the wall around my heart to even think about forgiving?" These are questions that only I can address, and deep down, I know the answers. The upset that disturbs my peace is a signal that I'm at choice: to forgive or not to forgive, to let go or cling to pain, to move on with my life or stay stuck in the grievance story that keeps playing itself out in my head.

Even if my most deeply held beliefs have been shattered by someone else's actions, I can ask, "Am I willing to turn over my peace to this person? Is it worth it? Am I willing to let *their* actions keep me from living *my* life the way I want to live it?"

Working with forgiveness is a sacred process. Honoring the betrayal gives it a chance to be heard, which is important. Part of my very human experience includes the emotions that surface when I've been hurt. Forgiveness doesn't mean that I shouldn't feel that pain. In reality, it's pretty hard to ignore it! It's what I do with the pain that matters. If I hold onto it, I become hostage to it. So what's next? How will I set myself free?

I am here by divine appointment, born of a loving Creator so that it can show up in the world through me, as me. The nature

of the Infinite One is wisdom, peace, love, and joy. Wherever I am
. . . whatever is going on in my life . . . wisdom, peace, love, and
joy exist at my very core. Forgiveness offers me the opportunity
to become centered in my core and know myself at a deeper level.
I've practiced forgiveness in all kinds of scenarios, as opportunities
show up almost daily. Here is what I've found to be helpful:

When my peace is disturbed for any reason, I give myself time
to be with the experience. I find a quiet space, either alone or with
someone I trust, and give myself plenty of time to move through
the process. Keeping tissues handy (tears are great healers!) I don't
deny the feelings that come up. Instead I let them speak.

What do they have to say? I let them be felt.

What sensations do they bring to my body?

Are images of past painful memories triggered? What are those
triggers?

I don't try to understand any of it; instead I just let it all come
forward to be noticed and felt, without judgment. I do my best to
get out of my head and into my emotional, feeling body.

With complete acceptance for *what is* in the moment, I just let it
be. My goal is to be willing to let the disturbing event lead me to
unconditional acceptance of myself, exactly as I am, in all of life's
chaotic commotion, without trying to justify, understand or control
anything.

When I feel like I have completely experienced the emotions
around the incident, I sit in silence until I can feel the peace of my
true nature bringing calm to my pounding heart, soothing my
frazzled nerves and holding me in its love. I am touching my core,
my authentic self . . . the greatest Love of all . . . within me, as me.

The same process works for self-forgiveness.

Like many of us, the most difficult person to forgive is me. Why?
Because it means I have to let go of the guilt I'm so used to carrying
around. When I've done something wrong I feel ashamed. I haven't

lived up to who I think I should be. I hope others won't see the "real" me, the one who committed the wicked deed.

In my self-forgiveness process I ask, "What ill feelings am I harboring against myself for something I've said, done, or even thought about, whether it's big or very small? Is my culpability stopping me from showing up honestly and authentically in the world?" Only I can answer these questions. If I've beat myself up long enough, I follow the same process that I use to forgive others. I stick with it and may need to repeat the process more than once, as releasing self-blame seems to be a stickler. The end result is self-acceptance, self-forgiveness and freedom!

I'm the one who decides to how I'll see and respond to any event—I can become the victim or the hero of my story. My forgiveness doesn't mean that I accept poor behavior or that I now trust that person. Using my own good sense, I know whether or not it's a good idea to have any contact with them at all. My forgiveness is about getting on with my own life, which may or may not include a relationship with the person I've forgiven.

Every single time I know I must forgive is a reminder that within me I have everything it takes to let go, fly and be free! In allowing myself to feel the feelings, I experience acceptance. In being willing to be healed, healing occurs. Resentment, animosity and guilt are replaced with serenity, joy and a new zest for life. Whereas forgiveness may have started out as a practice, it may just lead to a new way of being in the world, letting the peace and power of my true self lead the way.

It's easy to get caught up in circumstances and use them to define me. At every moment, I have the option to reach for a higher vibration, one that releases that which is holding me hostage. With every single choice to forgive, those old walls around my heart come tumbling down.

Just like everything else, forgiveness is a choice that can become a way of life. Choosing forgiveness offers true healing, freedom from the pain of the past. The walls around my heart begin to crack, crumble and fall because they're no longer held together by the glue of my stored angst, shame, judgment and blame.

When I forgive, I'm released from feelings of victimization. Yes, that thing still happened, but I'm no longer its victim. Although the event is still part of my story, it's no longer the underlying script that creates my tomorrows. Today my forgiveness begins a brand new page on the story of my life, with a brand new *me* as the hero!

~

Forgiveness is my choice, freeing me from the pain of the past. Letting go of victimization, I am now the hero of my story!

Following My Inner Wisdom

I don't have to be enlightened to be peaceful and happy. Heck, I don't even have to know what I'm doing! All that's needed is to be open to the idea that *something within me* does know what to do. Solutions to daily challenges are created because I believe they exist, even if I can't see them now. Anyone can know this—people from any background or religion, or no religion at all. *Something* is guiding them, and when they act on it, they are in the flow of Life itself.

At first, the discovery of my inner wisdom was all about emotional trust. At the end of my marriage, terrified about leaving and yet knowing that staying was no longer an option, I needed help walking through fear, standing on my own, and getting out from under my shell of codependence. I turned to my inner wisdom, practiced paying attention, and got the guidance I needed. It was emotional proof that something within me knew what was needed and knew how to do it. I learned to follow divine direction because if left to my logical human thinking I was definitely up a creek without a paddle!

Then I realized that my growing faith in my God and in myself was creative. Knowing that my life was about to change big-time, I kept a journal about what I wanted in my life. Every evening I'd visualize what my new life might look like: colorful flowers in pots, green houseplant of every shape and size, me sitting on the couch reading a book and sipping tea, pale colored walls, a feeling of tranquility. Several months later I read my journal entries and realized that everything in that journal was now a reality in my life! It was a different kind of proof—physical proof that behind the scenes, the universe was creating on my behalf.

Believe that you're in the flow of Life's goodness, that in every instance you are being divinely guided. Let your own experience prove that your own inner wisdom is trustworthy. Surrendering to divine direction, you'll find the courage to follow it. Your growing faith will bring about blessings that you never could have imagined!

~

In every moment, in each situation, something within me knows what to do. I follow that inner guidance and move forward in faith.

Metamorphosis

Fuzzy caterpillars fill up on tasty plants, sustenance for the changes that come with metamorphosis and the resulting ability to fly free as butterflies. As a human being, I fill up on life experiences, sustenance for the changes that come with awakening to the strength and beauty of who I truly am—a spiritual being having a human experience. Every situation adds to my personal metamorphosis. Whatever's going on in this moment is important.

One of my favorite pastimes is seeing the face of God everywhere—in the trees, stop-lights, the walls of my townhouse, the air I breathe. It exists in rodent holes dug deep in the fields where tiny babies sleep. It's in the forest soil that nurtures the roots of giant redwoods while at the same time making space for ferns to take root on the forest floor. It exists in day care centers, gas stations, dog kennels, hospitals, churches, and prisons. Everywhere . . . at all times . . . in all things . . . Love is fully present. When I focus on any one thing and know it's made of God-stuff, I'm centered in the experience and my heart overflows with wonder. Have you ever stood under a tree and looked up to see the filtered rays of the sun shining through the branches? That's what Love does. It shines its light into the present moment so that we'll notice it's there.

As the Beloved leads the way, my capacity for awareness and compassion grows stronger every day. I no longer ignore the neighbor's cat but instead tell her hello. I don't slam doors—I close them. I leave earlier so I can enjoy traveling time. I help insects and spiders find their way back outside when they show up inside my home. Life is gentler today, and my metamorphosis is in full swing!

∽

*As I see the face of God in all things, my heart overflows
in wonder. Life is gentler today, and I am gentler in it.*

Moving Through Fear

How many times have I turned my back on a something as simple as trying something new, reconnecting with an old friend or asking someone for help because of old stuff that told me I can't, it won't work, I'll look silly and I shouldn't even try? "Can't" is a tool fear uses to keep me tightly boxed into what's familiar, where I live the same life, thinking the same thoughts, with the same results I've always had.

Here's where the God of my understanding comes in. I feel that divine nudge from the part of me that knows the joy of freedom. It whispers, "Break free! Do something new! Take a chance!" I'm reminded that as a child I took lots of chances, like learning to ride a bike, attending my first sleepover, being stoic for visits to the doctor and dentist, attending a new school and making friends on the playground. As a child almost everything is new, so moving forward is mandatory. Still, it's scary. What if it doesn't turn out? What if I look stupid? But like other children I did it—I put one foot in front of the other and moved forward anyway, and eventually I got to the other side. Slowly I learned that I was more courageous than I had believed myself to be.

As I reflect on all the challenges I've already moved through, I see now them as accomplishments. How I view my life is up to me. It's my choice to notice and value every single time I moved through fear and give myself credit for doing so. Today I give myself credit for my everyday courage. Being courageous isn't always about running into a burning building or confronting a bully—instead it shows up in the daily decisions that enhance my life.

There have been times when I've needed to change doctors or dentists, let go of a service provider like a handyman or woman, housecleaner, or a technical support person. Sometimes they are people I've gotten to know over many years, but now it's time to part ways. It's my job to lovingly and clearly acknowledge that it's time to part ways. Not taking action causes all kinds of uncomfortable feelings—beating myself up for putting it off, inviting complications that just keep escalating. My guilt hangs out like a black cloud in the back of my mind. My courage to take action moves me out from under the cloud and into the sunshine.

Everyday courage shows up on my calendar. Do I really want to attend that traditional family function, the cocktail party on Friday night with business associates or the new horror flick with my movie friends? What would happen if I said no? My everyday courage calls for me to accept activities that feel good and let go of those that don't. Once I begin saying no to what doesn't serve me, I get on a courage-roll. Taking my life back feels good, even if underneath there are people grumbling to me or about me because I'm not doing it their way. In the end, the only one who can take responsibility for my life is me. I own my happiness or my lack of it. I'm the one who can make it happen.

~

Every day I have the courage to make decisions that are in my best interest.

Learning From Nature

Nature reminds me that nothing is stagnant, that everything changes all the time. The cycles of the seasons are a perfect example. Autumn is magical. Somehow the leaves know it's time to turn to brilliant shades of gold and squirrels begin hiding their bounty of seeds and nuts. Autumn breezes partner with the falling leaves to spin and twirl in a joyous ballet. The rays of the sun seem to shift and sway with wind-swept clouds. As the wind picks up, dogs find fun everywhere, whether it's chasing a stick, a ball, or their own tail! Delighting in the crackling of dried leaves under my feet, I join in the magic of autumn's fun as I feel the shift in energy that fall brings.

As the weather continues to cool into winter, activity quiets. Nature's creatures find simple pleasure in the moment, just because it feels good. Cats warm themselves by windows, catching the rays of sunshine peeking out from behind gray clouds. Plants go dormant. Forest animals hibernate. Trees look bare while in reality they harbor new life, as tiny buds grow within the safety of the branches that hold them. It's a time of quiet, allowing the space for renewal to take place. In winter I hunker down, taking time to reflect on where I am in my life, allowing space for my inner wisdom to offer ideas for contemplation.

The heralding of spring marks new beginnings. The buds hidden within tree branches burst open by the warmth of a sunny spring day. Tiny shoots of green break through their shells, reaching for the sun past the soil that has nurtured them all winter long. Flowers of every shape and hue open to the light in all their splendor. Animal babies take their first look at the world around them, exploring the life that they've been given. I too, feel the urge to move forward, investigating the ideas that I mulled over during the winter. Spring is a time for action!

Summer is filled with activity—caterpillars munching their way through leaves in preparation for transformation in the chrysalis, soon to become the butterflies that visit our gardens. The calls of crickets, cicadas and frogs fill the night air. Gardens overflow with produce that graces our tables and delights our taste buds. Fruit trees become an invitation for feasting on their tasty bounty. As summer temperatures rise by mid-day, activity tends to slow down, as many living beings seek the cool of the shade offered by nearby trees. Summer is a time of relishing in the abundance of goodness life has to offer!

Finally, as the end of summer approaches, the nights are a little longer, the weather begins to cool, and migrations get into full swing, a reminder that change is ever-present. Change is normal and natural for me, too. Just as animals and birds know when to prepare for the next phase of life, I listen to the whisperings of my own inner wisdom, signaling next steps. Setting my intention to be divinely guided, to live abundantly and thrive, I step into the flow of life as part of the tapestry of Nature's divine masterpiece.

~

The magic of the cycles of nature reminds me to join in the glory of each season, for I am part of the tapestry of Nature's divine masterpiece.

From Chaos to Peace

Chaos is defined as "a state of utter confusion or disorder." In reality, chaos is everywhere, a part of life that comes with change. It's what I do with it that counts—will it add to my stress or build my faith?

My life can be going along well when all of a sudden something happens—a disturbing phone call, an unexpected bill, a flat tire, a canceled airline flight, an unforeseen project at work, a disagreement with a friend, a loved one's drama, an illness or accident. If I go onto auto-pilot my first response is, "Oh no!" and fear sets in. Then I remember that my response to the chaos is creative. If I allow myself to get swallowed up in the chaotic experience, my stress goes sky-high. That stress sends a signal to the universe that says, "Here is someone who has an attraction to stress, so send her some more." The signal I want to send is, "Here is someone who has an attraction to inner peace, so send her some more of that." I have an important role in the situation. I am the one who can, to the best of my ability, control my response to the chaos. I am the one who can invite inner peace back into my life.

My first job is to release the whole process to the God of my understanding, "Here, I give this situation to you. Guide me through it, step by step. Help me like myself in the situation. When I forget, I'll lean on you to help me remember the truth of who I am, that at my core I am peace, harmony, clarity and balance, everything that it takes to get me through this. I willingly surrender this situation to you so that I can once again feel my own peace." This keeps me focused on what's important instead of the challenge that can so easily rob me of the inner peace I deserve.

My second job is to let go of the way the chaotic experience needs to turn out. This is a biggie because it means I can't try to control it. Instead of making assumptions about what needs to happen, I can listen for divine direction and take action from that perspective, which is always for the best and highest good for all concerned. I can do my part while I let others do their part, which will be a constant reminder to take my hands off the steering wheel.

My third job is to let go of my expectations for how the others should do their part. It's so easy to think I know what they should do and when they should do it, making up a scenario about how it should all turn out. Instead, I once again turn to the Beloved for comfort, support, strength and guidance in order to let the whole thing play itself out.

My fourth job is to stay in gratitude for everything that I already have — running water, clothes in my closet, food in my stomach, the weather (no matter what it is), the ability to choose, the willingness to learn, a God that adores me. My gratitude grounds me, expands my inner peace and also opens a creative space for miracles to occur within the chaos around me.

My fifth job is to stick with it. I'm not always going to be peaceful. There will be times when the urge to control may spill over into the situation and make it worse. I may tell someone what they should be doing and how they should do it. Choosing peace instead of stress takes time, patience and a lot of practice. When I forget I learn from it, apologize where necessary and get back on track. Although inner peace is part of my spiritual core, consciously bringing it into my everyday human experience involves determination and perseverance to stay the course. It takes a willingness to commit to a healthy balance of humility, as I surrender my need to control everything, and self-kindness, as I practice being gentle with myself in the process.

Because chaos is part of the flow of change, it is my constant reminder to be who I want to be in the world. Chaotic situations can be my teachers and I can be a willing student. I didn't choose the situation, but here it is anyway. Because I'm always at choice, I can accept it and do my best as I move through it, or I can resist it and add a whole lot of stress to my life. It really is up to me, and I am worth whatever it takes to choose inner peace.

∼

When a chaotic situation occurs, I choose inner peace.

Joining the World

When I judge another's lifestyle, I create a border. When I'm a critical of a friend's perspective or behavior, a wall goes up. When I find fault with the way a person looks, the wall gets higher. Soon I've boxed myself into a very lonely place where the only one who's right is me. Willingness sets a solid foundation for action. In Al-Anon I became willing to make amends to those I had harmed before I actually made my apologies—it paved the way for the honesty, humility, courage, and respect needed to take responsibility for my choices. Once I became willing, following through was easier, and I learned that I was worthy of change.

I recognize that every single person who has ever been in my life has been there for a reason. Within each relationship has been something for me to learn in order to grow into the person I want to be. It's my opportunity to accept more completely, forgive more freely and love more fully. Each person is a blessing brought to me by a God that adores me.

I know now that I matter in the world, with dreams to be realized and joy to be lived. Humility, forgiveness and freedom are my new friends, teaching me to say yes to my heart. I've broken down the walls, cast aside the borders, lightened up, let go and joined the world! My new normal is love.

~

Gratefully, I know I matter in the world today. As I say yes to my heart, I step into the joy that's meant to be lived!

Chapter 9

I Am Changing

ONCE I UNDERSTOOD that my thoughts were creating my life, some of my beliefs and old ways of moving through the world popped up for consideration. Instead of just automatically assuming that the beliefs were true and my actions correct, I started challenging them, "Is this belief true today, or do I believe it just because I've always believed it? Is it in my best interests to allow this belief to guide my life with the same results I've always gotten?"

Forging a New Path

I started looking at my everyday life with fresh eyes. My inner wisdom kept whispering, "What do *you* want today? Today's a new day and you're a new you. What's important to you now?" I, who had been trained to always put others first, was supposed to consider what *I* wanted! It was uncomfortable to even think of such a thing. My ego-mind replied with, "You're being selfish. Who do you think you are? Do you think the world revolves around you?" I was bucking fifty years of thinking that told me that I was to put others first—it was the woman's job. I watched my mom do it, just as she had watched her mom do it. It wasn't so much verbalized as it was role modeled.

One of the first in-my-face challenges took place at the dining room table. I had joined the ranks of making sure everyone else had the best pieces of meat or the best portions of food and I'd take what's left. That's what a good mom does, right? I loved watching my family enjoy the finest because I wanted them to be happy! I had no idea that we could all enjoy the food equally. Instead I was modeling, "The mom puts herself last," for my children. Happily, they have seen through this old model and are living very different lives today.

Learning to value myself put me in brand new territory. It was clear that I had my own personal work cut out for me as I bucked a lifetime of cultural and familial training. Nothing about valuing my own self-worth and self-love came naturally. Setting boundaries were terrifying. Disappointing others by not playing my traditional role tore at my heart. But still, Divine Love kept nudging me forward, assuring me that we all matter, no one more important than another, no one person able to fix another. We all have our own path to follow, and it was time that I allow my own path to emerge.

One day an image came into my mind. I saw myself standing in a field of tall waist-high grass. My job was to forge a new path through the grass. It was *my* path. I needed to decide where to take the first step. The idea seemed daunting until I remembered that I wasn't alone. Standing in the field of grass I closed my eyes, allowed my mind and body to relax, and paid attention to the divine guidance that was within me. "Which way do I go?" I asked. Soon I felt the urge to turn slightly to my right, take one step forward, and start there. That's what I did. Taking one step forward, I could feel the grass resist, pushing against the intrusion of the weight of my body. In the past I would have stepped back off of the path, feeling responsible for the dent in that glorious free-standing grass. I would have simply stayed in the middle of the field, going nowhere, making sure I didn't cause waves. With the gentle assurance that it was safe to move forward . . . that I could buck those old beliefs that kept me playing small . . . I took one step at a time. I felt the resistance, practiced being okay in it, and then took the next step.

Every time I let go of a belief that belonged to my previous way of being, I took a step forward. As I practiced taking care of me, no matter how well I did it, I gained momentum. Each time I let go of someone's response to the changes in me, I could feel my power. As I trusted my own intuition, my faith grew. I realized that the resistance of the grass beneath my feet mirrored my resistance to my own evolution. Slowly it became easier.

Today I let others forge their own paths. I have no need to tell them which way to go or how to do it. I remember what it's like to stand in the middle of that field and learn to trust that the path will make itself clear. It's up to each of us to discover the strength and glory of our ability to walk our path, one step at a time.

~

I easily move through any resistance to change in order to walk my own path.

I'd Be Happy if . . .

Fill in the blank. I'd be happy if _____. So many choices! I'd be happy if I had a partner, if my partner would change, if my partner really loved me. I'd be happy if I had more money, a house of my own, a new car, a good job, a healthy body. I'd be happy if my family wasn't so dysfunctional, my loved ones got their act together, or the person who hurt me apologized. I'd be happy if I hadn't done the horrible things that make me feel ashamed, if I could kick my addiction, or if I had the guts to apologize to all the people I've hurt. I'd be happy if I could learn to love myself.

The human experience can be full of joy, and it can also be a melting pot of unfulfilled needs and regrets. The frustration, anger, fear, sorrow and remorse that they stir up can make us miserable! Looking for happiness outside of ourselves becomes our personal path to misery. As have many others, I've discovered that my happiness is an inside job. If I count on someone else to do what I want them to do in order for me to be happy, I'm setting myself up to be disappointed. It takes a lot of personal will power to practice knowing that I can be positive and happy no matter what's going on in my life. It takes faith, patience and endurance to practice positivity. It takes a sense of self-worth and self-love to be willing to be happy and peaceful.

Giving up misery brings my focus back to Love as the only option. When I ignore the behavior of some of those closest to me instead of allowing them to push my buttons, I'm detaching with love. The same is true when I let them fail instead of trying to save them—their life belongs to them. They will learn from their mistakes or not. They will turn their life around or not. With loving detachment, I can accept them as they are and let their journey be whatever it's going to be. I can also change the way I think about them, making a decision to concentrate on their positive aspects, which I've completely ignored by zeroing in on their negative actions. This sets into motion a whole new positive energy of optimism instead of negativity. With an open, upbeat heart I can hold them in my prayers, knowing that their Higher Power is right where they are, loving them unconditionally. I visualize the energy of Divine Love all around them and within them, holding them in every moment of every day. They can respond to this great Love or not because their life belongs to *them*.

Letting others live their own lives leaves much more time for me to concentrate on mine. When I make positivity and happiness my focus, it changes my energy. I have time to look for what's wonderful about life! I use my new freed-up time to hang out with people who uplift me and engage in activities that bring me pleasure. Soon I discover that I'm attracting others who are happy! I begin to notice the positive things about *me*, and my self-esteem improves. My awesomeness starts shining its light! Life's goodness starts coming my way. My body starts to feel better, an offer for a new job comes my way, and suddenly I no longer need that apology. When I begin to heal in one aspect of my life, it positively affects every aspect of my life. I choose my own happiness. I am worth my own time and attention.

~

I create my own happiness, one choice at a time. My awesomeness shines!

Eat the Ice Cream

When Mom was in her early 90s I took her to one of her many doctor appointments. She had recently moved into an assisted living facility where ice cream was served for dessert after dinner. Noting that she was putting on a bit of weight she confessed, "They serve ice cream every day, and I love it! I know it's not good for me, but I keep eating it." The doctor (bless his heart) replied, "People do without the things they love their whole lives in order to live as long as you've lived. Eat the ice cream!"

We humans have a tendency to put ourselves down for not measuring up to who we think we should be. There's a balance between healthy eating and occasional indulging, learning from informational documentaries and laughing at silly movies, completing a task and pitching the whole thing to do something fun instead. Isn't it time we give ourselves a break? If we know we're basically on course, can we allow ourselves some leeway without making it wrong? Can we work with our human imperfections without running away from them?

When I'm okay with my over and under indulgences, including days of getting absolutely nothing done and moments of having no awareness of which way I'm going, I let go of the need to be perfect. As spiritual beings having a human experience, I'm learning to honor the human experience. It's often unrealistic, disorganized and impractical. It asks us to accept ourselves, warts and all. It reminds us that sometimes it's okay to eat the ice cream and when we do, enjoy every single mouthful!

~

I lovingly accept all of me, striking a balance with my human imperfections.

Healthy, Loving Relationships

When I have a need that's not being met, it sets off a chain reaction that catches my attention. Thoughts about it keep popping up in my mind. I can feel it in my gut—something's missing. Everywhere I look I see evidence of what I want but don't have. If I don't address the need it becomes magnified. I'm at choice—either do something about it or add it to my "I'm a victim" list. Clearly it's time for action!

It really is all about me. The outside conditions of my life won't change until I tackle my inner work. If I want healthier, more loving relationships, I first have to become healthier and more loving. The primary person I must address is *me*. What do I love about myself? I make a list, the longer the better. It's tempting to downplay my loveable qualities because I'm so used to seeing my less-than-loveable qualities. The problem is that when I focus on myself negatively, my energy gives out negative vibes, which isn't very conducive to attracting loving, healthy relationships. In fact, that self-critical negativity is what likely attracted the undesirable relationships that are in my life now.

There's no way around it—if I want to change this aspect of my life, I have some internal healing to do. If needed, I work with a spiritual counselor, a therapist, support group, 12-step sponsor or a trusted friend. Am I worth the time and effort it takes to do the work? Am I deserving of having healthy, loving relationships? You bet I am! Once I begin to remember that, the healthy vibration of my new-found self-acceptance, self-worth and self-love will attract others who are feeling good about themselves, too. We won't have a need to gossip or complain about our lives because we're doing our best not to gossip or complain about ourselves.

Healthy, loving relationships will begin to show up in my life as the magnetic energy of my new thoughts and feelings create a pathway to the new, healthy, lovable me. At the same time, some of my less-than-healthy relationships will start to fall away. We're no longer a fit, not because I'm suddenly better than they are, but only because I've come to a fork in the road and am taking a new path. There is no right or wrong, instead there's only change. Sometimes it's tempting to try to hang onto those relationships as they have been part of my life for so long, but when the process of separation from 'what was' takes place, I owe it to myself to allow it to happen. The universe is on my side, doing its part to bring me into alignment with the happiness that healthy relationships offer. My job is to go with the flow instead of resisting it.

The process of letting go of my old way of being in the world takes time. I make it a top priority. Sometimes I'll do it well and sometimes I'll blow it, making a muddle of things. It's all part of the process. I'll stick with it because I choose to be healthy and loving. I choose to know myself as a person who has healthy, loving relationships. I choose to *be* the love that I am.

~

I have healthy, loving relationships, beginning with my relationship with me.

Practicing Happiness through Meditation

Each day is an opportunity to practice happiness. I am a powerful creator! Today I can make the decision to give myself the gift of my own time as I explore the happiness that is within me. It doesn't cost a thing, and it's full of the greatest riches! Even if I'm new to the practice of meditation, I will commit to spending five or ten minutes each morning and evening sitting quietly, with no expectation as to the results. I may begin with a spiritual reading or a short prayer, acknowledging the presence of Spirit within and around me, and then just be quiet. Thoughts will come and go—that's okay. I'll keep coming back to the quiet. Over time, as I consistently practice, I'll come away renewed, with a greater sense of Life's goodness and my part in it.

Love, peace, prosperity, health and joy are already given to each of us. We get to choose whether to accept them or not. When I quit complaining, I accept peace. When I appreciate all that I have, I accept prosperity. When I let myself or another off the hook, I accept love. When I realize that I'm loved unconditionally by a God that adores me, I accept joy. Today I accept my good.

I'm worth the gift of my own time, the awareness of my true self and the happiness that is my nature. I am Life's gift to the world, and discovering that is a glorious thing!

~

Happiness is within me, part of my spiritual nature. Each day I spend time renewing the gift of my own happiness.

Taking Responsibility for My Prosperity

Owning my life, taking full responsibility for my happiness, fosters prosperity. With appreciation for what I already have, I pay my bills with a heart filled with gratitude. How blessed I am to live in a country where gas is available for my car, where I can flip a switch to fill a room with light, turn on a faucet to get running water, and have a credit card company that trusts me enough to loan me money to make purchases ahead of time. My bills are reminders of my blessings!

Believing in my worthiness to prosper, it's easier to take care of the business of my life, bringing the best of who I am to my daily affairs. I tend to wear clothes that make me feel good, straighten my home before leaving for the day, and tip generously when I'm out. I return phone calls, walk the dog, take the garbage out, fold the laundry and wash the dishes with gratitude for the good they bring to my life. Grateful for the awareness that my life is worthwhile, I let it show in how I move through my day. The universe responds to my feelings of thanksgiving, and I get more for which to be grateful. My life prospers in ways I never even imagined because my feelings of worthiness and gratitude have opened the door to let prosperity in.

~

With a happy heart, I take full responsibility for my happiness, knowing that my gratitude for what I have and who I am invites the joy of prosperity into my life.

Owning My Life

As my faith grows, I've become more enthusiastic about life. Everything changes when I remember that I'm not alone, that an invisible Presence knows who I am, is ever-present and wants me to be happy. When I am willing to quit trying to control the world and be guided by Love itself, my life flows a lot more smoothly. Things work out on their own without my stressing about them. What a relief!

Believing in a God of my understanding has led to believing in me. Knowing that I'm loved just the way I am has led to self-acceptance. Even on days when I've made one mistake after another, that great Love still thinks I'm absolutely splendid! It sure makes it easier to be okay with me when I know that the Power that created the universe is okay with me! It's an invitation to be gentle with myself as I learn and stretch and grow in this very human lifetime.

Believing in me has led to owning my life, stepping out into new experiences. Today I move past my comfort zone in order to do what's in front of me. My intuition tells me when to say yes and when to say no. My 'yes' comes from faith. Even if it's scary because it's brand new, I'm willing to walk through my fear and go for it! My God would never put me in a situation that isn't in my best interest. I trust that kind of divine attention today.

Making mistakes has shown me what doesn't work as I learn and keep moving forward. My goofs have become my teachers—they help me gather information so that I can begin to see a larger picture. Instead of taking my mistakes personally, they have become tools in my ever-expanding tool bag of learning. They keep me from taking my life so seriously, and for that I'm very grateful!

I'm always in the process of questioning the thoughts that keep surfacing in my head. Negative or positive? True or false? Helpful or not so much? I've discovered that the easiest way to let go of an old habitual thought is to adopt a new one. For instance, if I tend to make choices that I later regret, I can set my intention to make at least one conscious choice each day that feels right to me. That choice becomes a powerful affirmation of self-worth. With practice my new thoughts and actions will become my new way of life—I'm worthy of making choices that are right for me! If I'm starting to beat myself up about anything, I make a conscious decision to do something kind or fun for myself each day for the next week to get me back into the flow of self-care. Then that intention becomes a new habit, and off I go, living a life that honors me! I am the one who lives my life, and I intend to do it well!

~

Owning my life is brave! It's fun! It's new and creative!
Honoring myself, I do it well.

Breaking Out!

As a former elementary schoolteacher, I noticed a change as children emerged from Kindergarten and ventured into my first grade classroom. Their pre-kindergarten, high-spirited, confident "I can do it!" attitudes sometimes slipped into a hesitancy born from the possibility that their answer might be wrong. Even in Kindergarten children are expected to learn the rudimentary basics of reading, writing and math. Whereas some started school knowing how to read, others had never held a book in their hands. Looking around at their classmates, those brand new students began to compare themselves to others. As they walked into my classroom, I realized how much courage it took for them to offer their opinion, their thoughts, their reasoning and their ideas.

Today, I ask myself how often I have carried this same hesitancy into my life, not letting others see who I really am for fear that I may not be good enough. How often have I squashed the creativity that was alive in me as a little child dancing to my own inner music? How deep is the need to fit in and not stand out? In how many ways have I settled on a life that is less than vibrant and fulfilling because I've become accustomed to playing small?

It's time to break out! It's time to stand up and be noticed! It's time to color outside the lines and own my opinions, whether those around me agree or not. I was created as a divine ambassador of a Presence that knows itself through me, a Presence that is wise, creative, and joy-filled. Those same attributes are bubbling up within me all the time because they are me! Why am I squashing them down, dimming my divine light, when all along I have the power to shine the light of my magnificence in a way that is true for me alone?

When I taught little kids, we would sometimes read a book together, using it as an example. Then I'd invite them to create their own story, with their own characters. An inventive form of phonetic spelling allowed them to spell a word the way it sounded to them, so that the flow of their creativity wouldn't be stalled by trying to figure out the "correct" spelling. It was perfectly okay for the word "beautiful" to be spelled "booteful." When it came time to illustrate their story, there would invariably be students who thought they couldn't draw well enough. This was my favorite part! Heading up to the whiteboard I'd say, "Your character might look something like this." I'd draw an oval for a body, a circle for a head, and straight lines for arms and legs. Then I'd add some spiky or curly hair and call it good! Their response? "Oh, I can do that!" Then they would proceed to bring out their own rendition of the character of their choice. Animals could be pink or purple and tree leaves could be shades of the rainbow. Why not? Let creativity come alive! Voilà, their masterpiece was born!

Then came Back-to-School Night when their parents would ask, "What are you teaching our children? I looked at their book. This is not real life." I loved it! It was my opportunity to talk to the parents about the importance of dreaming, of letting imaginations expand, of not trying to blend into the established status quo. Back-to-School Night became a reminder that living life was more than getting ahead and the journey really does matter. I would ask, "How long has it been since you laid in the grass with your kids and watched the clouds go by? It's not a waste of time—it's good for your children and it's good for you! There's balance between work and play, correct spelling and phonetic "make it up" spelling, staying within the lines and creating rainbow trees, traditional after-school activities and goofing around." Parents listened, and the need to see their children get ahead became tempered with a renewal of the joy of simply enjoying their lives.

Today I'm learning to take my own words to heart. I lay in the grass and watch the clouds go by. I walk barefoot. I wade in streams. I draw pictures on notecards and send them to others for the sheer joy of it. I wear clothes that make me feel good. I sing out loud to songs on the radio, and if I don't know the words I make them up. I laugh at the antics of the neighbor's cat. I say hello to the tiny bits of green that make their way through the surface of the sidewalk. I write what's in my heart and don't fuss too much about correct grammar. In the morning I smile at the face in the mirror and laugh at my bed-hair. The joy of life is within me, and I intend to live it!

~

With childlike delight I'm breaking out, enjoying the world around me and the creativity that overflows from me.

The Power of My Enthusiasm

There have been days when I've been so excited about what I was doing that I completely lost track of time. I hadn't even stopped to eat, and I love to eat! And then I looked at what I had accomplished and my heart is full. It feels wonderful, and in it I feel truly alive.

Experience has shown me that when my enthusiasm is evident and sustained, the universe picks up on that passionate energy, diving right in to join the party. New, creative ideas come to mind, solutions to potential stumbling blocks appear, next steps become clear, and a joyful, motivated feeling compels me to keep going.

It's incredibly important to make time to do the things that I'm enthusiastic about every day. Listed are several reasons:

- It feels good! Even if I work at a job that's less than thrilling, I know that later that day I'll engage in the activity that I love, and my happy anticipation carries me through my day. It helps me stay on the bright side of everything I do and each interaction I have. I may even get up early to start my day with this activity, filling me with the joy that sets me up for an optimistic, productive day.

- When I feel good, the energy of my positive feelings calls others to me who are in the same "feeling good" vibrational frequency. It also invites feel-good situations into my life. The universe is alive, responding to how I show up. Like a magnet I attract other people and circumstances that match my energy. It pays to be happy!
- When a challenge hits, it's simpler to get to the feel-good place. It's easier to remember how it feels when my enthusiasm carries me forward because I engage in that activity daily. That same sustained positive energy can help me move productively through the challenge, staying open to learning from each mistake without getting mired in it, opening the door to resolutions.

The power of my enthusiasm sustains me as I move through my day, as well as those times when life-challenges hit. It's a way of being that I practice in my daily activities. Sustained, my zest for life grows and flourishes, bringing joy to every area of my life.

〜

Each day I engage in at least one activity that engages my enthusiasm for life.

Putting Guilt and Shame in Perspective

Shame and guilt aren't part of my spiritual make-up. Instead they are very much a part of my human experience. They seem to originate as a cultural thing, just as values, traditions and ways of living differ from culture to culture. Just look at the wide variations of traditional ceremonies—weddings and funerals in some cultures are dignified, emotions subdued, quietly honoring timeless traditions. In other cultures weddings and funerals are boisterous, out-of-the-box demonstrative affairs.

Families tend to settle into neighborhoods with others who

share the same general cultural beliefs, reinforcing the opinions in the minds of children as they grow up. Youngsters become indoctrinated with "this is the way we do it" within their own families, then reinforced as they get to know other children and their families. Stepping out of the norm sends a message that they've done something wrong, so the concern of shame and guilt help keep them in line.

Within each individual family are the combinations of cultural experiences brought to the table by the heads of the family. Whether a parent or guardian was raised in a very strict household or one so loose that children practically raised themselves, their upbringing influences how they raise their children. In some households expressing anger or other negative emotions is frowned on, while others let negative emotions fly in loud verbal outbursts. If a child responds to any situation with an emotion or action that doesn't fit the expected norm, they are in the wrong. Shame and guilt take hold in earnest.

As a child, the fear of disappointing my parents stopped me from doing a lot of things, which worked most of the time—I wanted my parents to be proud of me. As I grew older, the lure of peer pressure and the need for independence set in, and I started purposely doing things I knew were wrong. When I was seventeen I started smoking—it was the cool thing to do. I'll never forget my mom, who was upset with my decision, saying, "Well, if you have to smoke, do it at home. I don't want to ever see you walking down the street with a cigarette in your hand."

To my parents appearances meant everything. I was careful not to embarrass them with my smoking for fear of disappointing them even further, but their displeasure didn't stop me from indulging. Twenty years later I quit smoking, largely because as a teacher it had become so frowned upon that the societal peer pressure left me ashamed enough to quit. Sometimes guilt nudges me in a better direction . . ..

When I was twenty-one I became pregnant, filling me with a conglomeration of feelings. I was packed with guilt, terrified to tell my parents, knowing they'd be disappointed along with that whole what-would-people-say thing. And yet I loved the baby's father. Most of all, I was thrilled to be having a baby! Trying to save face, my mom stepped into action, making the best of the situation. In those days pregnancy required an automatic "shotgun" wedding. Since I was in the middle of a college semester at the time, my mom took care of everything. She arranged a beautiful, intimate family wedding, hoping that the timing discrepancy between the wedding date and birth date would go unnoticed. For me, once I was married, all feelings of shame were lifted—I was now legitimate, married to a man I loved and we were having a baby!

As a parent, I found myself falling into many of the same cultural behaviors that were modeled for me as a child. When my children were toddlers, I went to my first Al-Anon meetings (Al-Anon is a 12-step program for family and friends of alcoholics). I told no one because it was imperative for everyone to believe that our lives were just fine—that *what-would-people-think* thing.

Then I discovered a stumbling block—there was a problem with Al-Anon. I was an atheist and 12-step programs are based on finding a Higher Power. Yikes! What was I supposed to do with that? I kept looking for a meeting that wasn't based on building a relationship with a Higher Power, and of course I was unsuccessful, so I stopped going. For the next twenty-five years or so, under the veil of shame that people would find out and judge us, I pretended that all was well. It wasn't until our 30th anniversary that I went back to Al-Anon, finally willing to creep out from behind my wall of deceit to allow myself the gift of recovery.

One year later I knew I needed to leave my marriage. Telling those I loved about the intended divorce was one of the hardest things I've ever done. I had done such a good job of faking it that most of my family had no idea. Finally coming clean was scary and at the same time, it was a huge relief. I could smell the scent of freedom in the air!

Since then I've learned a lot about how to put guilt and shame into perspective. Yes, they can stop me from acting inappropriately, but often they keep me from showing up authentically. No more codependent *everything's fine* when it's not. On the other side of guilt and shame lies the ability to say what I need and share what's truly in my heart. I like who I am, no matter what my life looks like. When an old guilty feeling creeps in I notice and ask, "What's this about?" Then I make a conscious decision as to what to do about it, knowing that shame and guilt are no longer options in the life I choose to live today.

~

Standing tall in my own authenticity, I release shame and guilt, holding my head up high, liking myself just as I am.

In the Middle of the Big Picture

There's always a bigger picture to any situation. The big picture is made up of small moments, each adding to the outcome of the full scope of our life. "This too shall pass" is true about the moment, and at the same time the way in which I deal with the moment will affect the outcome—the big picture. If I'm sitting in the dentist's chair, I'm part of the bigger picture of physical health. If I've overcome fear of the dentist just to be sitting in the chair, it's part of the big picture called courage. If I've adjusted my finances in order to make the dental visit possible, it's part of the big financial picture. If I've made the dental visit a priority because I believe I'm important enough to take care of my teeth, I've added positivity to the big picture of self-worth.

Change is ongoing, requiring a period of growth with a beginning, middle and end to each particular big-picture transition. By nature the middle—the in-between—lasts the longest. On my spiritual path the middle is where the work is done to get from where I am to where I want to be. For the new to begin, the old must end. In order for the old to end, I have to let it go. The middle is the letting-go part. It's where the unsure, uncomfortable, ever-changing I-messed-up-again, now-I'll-start-over becomes my daily practice. Understanding that there's a bigger picture helps me put my daily practice in perspective, and that's what the middle is all about.

When I seek to make conscious changes, choosing new behaviors is the beginning. Practicing is the middle. Self-mastery is the end. I won't always need to be so focused on applying new behaviors—after I get used to saying yes to what I want and no to what I don't want, it will start to come more naturally. But first I have to practice it in every conceivable situation. I must deal with my doubts, my fears and those old beliefs that keep rolling around in my head.

Being in the middle often leaves me feeling empty as I let go of the old without the ability to stand firm in the new. It's the slippery slope that goes along with the willingness to change. It's meant to challenge me. It's supposed to grow me. Every time I trust myself enough to take even the tiniest next step, my confidence flourishes. As I stick to it, even when I want to fall back into old behaviors, I recognize a courage and resilience that's new. I can feel myself approaching the ending because I grasp the fact that I'm a whole different person than the one who started that particular period of change! I'm up to the task of living the life I want to live, and the big picture of my life is now a lot shinier!

~

Being in the middle of the big picture challenges me to be the best I can be in each moment, knowing that every experience adds to the big picture of my life.

Chapter 10

I Am Free

HOW BIG IS DIVINE LOVE? It's really, really big! As it manages the entire universe, it extends into the vastness of my deepest, darkest fears to shine its light on each of them. This light of love has no need to change my fears—instead it simply wants them to know how loved they are. Period. Divine Love is uncomplicated, gentle and without an agenda. I get to decide how to respond to it. Because it has no agenda my response is always okay, accepted as is.

Love's Divine Attention

I find myself leaning in, paying attention to Love's message. My life becomes filled with the strength of accepted uncertainty as I allow myself to be led. Through me God as the universe is bringing about something new and forward-moving, which will be for the highest and best for everyone, because that's the way Love works.

Knowing how loved I am gives me the courage to go after what makes me happy. Love's divine attention helps me stand up for what's important to me and let go of what's no longer serving me. It invites me to live my life wholly and completely and for this I am grateful.

~

I turn toward Love's divine attention, discovering how very precious I am to the God of my understanding.

Taking Care of Myself

I was one of the world's best codependents until I discovered that God was real. The Beloved kept whispering, "I love you just as you are. You're my glorious one!" The more I paid attention, the more I believed it. If I was so glorious, why was I settling for the life that made others happy but left me feeling empty? Somehow I knew I was much more than the person I was pretending to be. I had no idea what my new life was to be, but I knew that if I paid attention to the divine direction of my inner wisdom, I would know as I went along.

In each situation I asked, "Is this for me or for someone else?" My gut reaction would tell me. If it was for me I went with it and patted myself on the back for taking care of myself. If it was for someone else at the expense of my own serenity I asked, "What will I do about it?" The answer would come to me as a powerful new thought—sometimes it was to say no, even though I knew my answer would cause a ruckus. Although rocking the boat was scary, it was empowering to say no anyway! It was time for people to see the change in me. I didn't need to discuss or defend my changes— my actions could speak for themselves.

I learned powerful tools for self-care in Al-Anon. One of them was what to do about phone calls from people who I really didn't want to talk to, but out of respect they needed a bit of my attention. It was suggested that when that person called I could say, "Hi Joe.

I have two minutes (or whatever amount of time I had previously decided upon). What's on your mind?" Then stick to it! "Time's up. Thanks for calling. Bye!"

I began to recognize when others were trying to make me feel guilty for changing. I realized that I had done the same with others in the past—using guilt was part of my need to control. Gently, I unhooked myself from any feelings of resentment or blame and, to the best of my abilities, sent that person a feeling of loving kindness instead.

It takes lots of practice to undo lifelong habits, and sometimes I don't do so well, but with every situation I apply what I'm learning, heal, and grow. The Beloved was right—I am its glorious one! I deserve my own love and respect.

~

In every situation I practice taking care of myself.
I deserve my love and respect.

Detaching with Love

One of the greatest gifts I can give myself is to detach with love. No longer do I need to worry, fret, nag and cajole, trying to get the other person to do what I think they should do. No more sleepless nights! Now I'll have time to do the things that make me happy, or maybe try something brand new like painting or creating a website or starting an organic garden. Just think of the inspired time I'll have because my head isn't encumbered with someone else's life!

In Al-Anon I learned about detaching with love. Coming from a place of respect, it was a whole new way to look at detachment. In my own life I don't want to be told how to live. Why would someone else want me to tell them how to live their life? My life finally became enough of a mess that I walked through the doors of recovery and found my Higher Power. The result? My life took off in a new direction that's amazingly creative, fulfilled and happy!

That wouldn't have happened without hitting my bottom. Am I going to rob someone else of their chance for happiness by trying to save them from hitting their bottom?

Detaching with love takes practice and perseverance, one situation at a time. I can listen to a friend's conversation without trying to change their mind or wait to respond to a text, email or phone message until I can do so with grace. I can watch the news without ranting about what's happening in the world. I can wait until I get a clear picture of what's going on at work before jumping in with my opinion, and only then offer my thoughts if asked. Daily practice becomes a habit, leaving a whole lot more time to discover activities that are fun for me and then do them. Detaching with love not only honors the other person, it honors me!

~

As I detach with love, I create a whole bunch of time to discover what makes ME happy!

Making a Difference

When humans hurt each other intentionally, it gives us cause to reflect about what's really important. The question many have asked is, "What's happening to humankind?" as we focus on the fear and horror created. Because we're each in the process of our own inner awakening, situations such as these gives rise to the questions, "What's my role in this situation? What can *I* do about it? What's *my* vision for the world? " These questions invite me to dig deep into my own heart for answers, taking me from a helpless feeling to a belief that I can be part of the solution.

With the eyes of awareness, I pay attention a situation that touches me emotionally—the one I most react to when I hear about it in the news. I look within for the answers to my questions. Then I act on those answers. My vision for the world creates a space for God to do what God does so well through me. Through me the

Beloved heals. Through me the world moves in a positive direction. If what I can do is pray, then I hold my most positive prayer for the highest good for all, never wavering. If I can join a committee, or write a letter, I do that. If I can plant a tree, send a check or become a volunteer, I do that. I make a difference in the world by holding the space for change and acting on it.

~

I hold a high vision for the world today, knowing that I make a difference. I'm part of bringing the highest and best good to all concerned.

Loving Kindness is Who I Am

I wipe the slate clean of negativity today. I focus on what's right in the world. I look for simple acts of kindness and read 'good news' stories. My conversations are upbeat, and I smile! Recently I was walking across the bank parking lot. A car rounded the corner; the driver saw me and stopped to let me pass. I grinned, waved, and trotted across. He smiled, waved and drove on. A simple thing really, and yet it was filled with joy and camaraderie, each of us feeling the positive effects of having come into each other's presence.

When I thank my bed for a restful night's sleep, the energy of my gratitude is a blessing to the world. When I prepare my food consciously, or slow down for merging cars, or let go of a resentment, I'm a blessing to the world. Kindness brings out the best in me. I can choose to be an unexpected blessing, even in the middle of an unwanted surprise. If someone is critical of me, I can meet them with a soft voice, a calm demeanor. If someone is impatient with me, I can stand tall in evenness of temper and grace. Loving kindness is who I am. As I go about my day as God's blessing, I uplift the vibration of the world, one simple kindness a time. Everyone wins!

~

*I joyfully wipe the slate clean of negativity, moving
through my day with a positive outlook and responding
to every situation with kindness.*

What Would Love Do Now?

I create an opportunity for transformation when I ask, "What would Love do now?" It opens up a space in me that's limitless—filled with potential and vast with wisdom. As I lean into the question I surrender to what's possible, without the need for any specific outcome.

Realizing I'm a place of peace and love if I choose to be, I practice in simple, everyday situations. I focus on sending love to everyone who shares the road with me, or stands in line with me, or sits in the doctor's waiting room with me.

The opposite of inviting Love in is complaining. How many times have I complained in my head about the people sharing the road, or the long line I'm standing in, or the extended wait in the doctor's office? This not only brings more negative energy into the situation, it sets me up for more negativity in the future. Just think of how often I've complained in my mind before I ever complained out loud! That's a lot of negative energy!

Reversing my tendency to complain is why I daily rehearse the opposite, "What would Love do now?" Because I've practiced asking the question and then acting on it, it's easier to get there when I'm in a challenging situation. Instead of jumping to fix it, defend my position, or complain, I silently ask, "What would Love do now?" I can feel myself relax as I hand it over to the part of me that knows what to do with it. I feel a quiet calm, which is usually an indication that I'm to wait and say nothing. If and when I'm to speak, I'll know when and what words to say. As I listen for divine guidance, I find myself relaxing, letting go of the need to control the situation. It gives me time to send positive energy to everyone involved, and my whole demeanor shifts. I become the watcher, seeing how Love will to do its thing. Sometimes challenges resolve themselves without me even saying a word! Miracles occur when I make the space for them.

~

By asking, "What would Love do now?" I create a space
for infinite possibility to do its good.

Personal Liberation

As my relationship with the Beloved has deepened, I've found myself seeking solitude and simplicity. It's much easier to feel the Presence when I'm not so busy accomplishing numerous "to-do" lists. Of course, we all have events and activities that need to be addressed. The question I asked myself was, "Is there anything that can be cut from my to-do list? What's really important to me and what isn't?" One of my most essential action tools has been learning to say "No" when I don't really want to do something and "Yes" when I do want to do it. For instance:

- I say no to most engagements where conversation consists of small talk.
- I say yes to activities where meaningful conversation takes place, one-on-one or small group interactions with a give and take of listening and learning from each other.
- I say no to spending lots of time chatting on the phone or texting just to see 'what's up' with others.
- I say yes to long periods of quiet time writing books and preparing Sunday messages. In the silence a sense of divine creativity flows through me that I never even knew I had, and it fills me with purpose.
- I say no to frequent shopping trips to buy the latest clothes, technology, or household goods.

- I say yes to frequent trips to donation facilities with articles that I no longer need and are sure to make someone else happy.

What about you? If you were to spend time considering what you say "Yes" to and what you say "No" to, would it match what is really important to you? If not, you can change your mind! Being consciously aware of where you spend your time and attention is powerful. Acting on it is liberating! Don't you think you are worth personal liberation?

~

I feel personal liberation by saying yes to what's important to me and no to what isn't.

Boundaries Benefit Everyone

As a toddler, "No!" came out of my mouth easily as I discovered that it was possible to alter the outcome of a situation in my favor. If I threw a big enough tantrum, sometimes I got my way. Something happened to that fierce, defiant independence as I got older and became acclimated to the expected behavior of the social structure I lived in. If I insisted on getting my way, others were disappointed in me . . . I wasn't getting along with the group . . . I was being selfish. I started to watch people from a child's perspective. Because I wanted to be accepted and loved, I learned how to make other's happy, pushing my wishes away. At the time it was worth it—others wanted to be around me, which made me happy. In reality I was learning to be a very good codependent, taking care of everyone else to the point that I didn't take care of myself. I had no idea how to balance the healthy give and take of relationships.

Once I discovered that God was real, all that changed. I learned that I was good enough as is, that I didn't need to please others to be accepted. Nor did I need to accept out-of-control behavior. Instead I could set boundaries as to what I would and wouldn't accept. I learned to lovingly make my desires known and then back them up with action. It was scary! At age fifty I was learning to speak up, knowing that people may walk away from me forever. I did it anyway because I was worth being in situations that were peaceful and happy. I no longer needed to settle for less.

Everyone gets to make their own choices. Setting boundaries helps me take responsibility for mine and lets everyone else take responsibility for theirs. I alone am responsible for my thoughts. I no longer need to turn them over to someone else just to keep the peace. My peace belongs to me. If my thoughts aren't peaceful, I'm the one who must examine them, see what's true and what isn't, and toss any that don't head me in the direction of peace. It takes rigorous attention to what's happening at any given moment, and because I'm no longer worried about taking care of everyone else, I have time to practice.

Setting boundaries allows me to love with a full heart, not one that's masking who I really am. It's easier to give love and to accept it. I can let others get close to me because I know who I am and what's important to me. If a situation comes up that causes me to be unsure, there's a wisdom within me that knows what to do. If a boundary needs to be set I'll articulate it and follow through with action. Coming from my full heart, the process is healthy, loving and clear: *That behavior crosses a line with me so I won't be part of it / participate in it.* It doesn't make the other person wrong or bad— instead it's about what I will and won't accept.

Unhealthy relationships and situations feel uncomfortable for a reason—they're indicators that I'm going in a direction that isn't good for me. At any given moment I can choose to head in a direction of self-respect. From that place of self-respect, I can offer respect to others as I allow them to live their lives while I live mine.

Every single time I set a healthy boundary, I send a message to the universe that says, "This is what I'll accept in my life." The universe picks up on the vibration of what I stand for and sends me more of what I *do* want in the world. In being willing to speak up, I stand for myself. My self-esteem grows as I realize that I'm worth the happiness that Life is trying to give me.

~

My healthy boundaries say yes to the life I choose for myself.

Faith in Time of Uncertainty

There have been many times when I didn't know what to do. Not wanting to make the situation worse, I sometimes became paralyzed and did nothing. Soon someone else would take charge and I'd be carried away with their solution. Sometimes it worked out, but often it didn't. I'd end up berating myself, "Why didn't I say something?"

There have been other times when I didn't know what to do and made up my own solution because it seemed better than nothing. Again, sometimes it turned out to be a good idea and other times it made things worse. Then I was filled with remorse.

Today I'm better at accepting uncertainty. I don't always have to know what to do and how to do it. Saying "I don't know" opens the door to the part of me that does know. My simple prayer becomes, "Tell me what to do." The answer will come when the time is right. In the meantime I get on with my life, enjoying every moment, filled with the faith that answered prayer will show up as the clarity needed to know what to do, how to do it and when to do it.

~

In times of uncertainty I turn to the part of me that knows what to do. With faith, I await the clarity I seek.

I Matter in the World

This moment is the perfect time for a new understanding—an awareness of just how much I matter in the world. What I think about, what I talk about, how I feel as I move through the day, all contribute to the evolution of humanity. I am much more important than I may realize!

What I choose for myself I choose for the world. When I'm fully attentive to whatever I'm doing, not only is my experience enriched, I'm send the vibration of purposeful awareness out into the world. At work, when I bring the gift of my skills to the task at hand, it feels good! I'm offering the best of myself to the situation. When I appreciate the skills of those around me, the energy of my appreciation uplifts everyone.

When I don't let someone else's comment push my buttons, I not only feel the inner strength of my non-reaction, I send that strength out into the universe. When I choose forgiveness for an unintentional misstep, the energy of my forgiveness touches the hearts of those who are hungry for it. When I'm as happy and fulfilled as possible, I uplift the consciousness of the universe.

When I'm grateful for what I have, my gratitude magnifies the energy of appreciation that can be felt across the seas. I look around me. Am I grateful for the face of a loved one, a hot shower, the first flower of spring, my good health, the company of my pet? Good! Let that gratitude put a smile on my face and warmth in my heart— the universe is better because of it.

As I begin to appreciate the money I do have (even if it's not a lot), my gratitude attracts abundance to me *and* shifts the prosperity consciousness of the world. When I dump old beliefs of lack and replace them with new beliefs of prosperity, I raise the vibration of success for the whole world. I become happy when I hear about another's good fortune, relishing the abundance contained in our ever-giving universe. My gratitude for any unexpected income reverberates throughout the cosmos, and a wave of prosperity gains momentum. My win becomes everyone's win!

I really do matter in the world. Every positive thought, each excited feeling, creates a consciousness of possibility that is a powerful force in the universe. My happiness is everyone's happiness! I'm going for it!

～

I matter in the world—the vibration of my happiness positively affects others.

Everything in My Life is For Me

I believe that everything in my life is somehow for me and never against me. With each situation, I'm given an opportunity to move out of my old thought patterns and habits of behavior to become more of who I want to be.

When I'm driving and sail through a series of green lights, fantastic! If I am stopped at every red light, that's good, too. I can use that time to be grateful that I have a car to drive, money for gasoline, and paved roads to take me to my destination.

If I step on the scale and the numbers look good, that's great! If I've put on a pound, I can see it as a reminder that I'm always at choice as to what I eat and how much exercise I get. Appreciating my very human body, I can choose to adjust as I move through my day. At the same time, I gently remind myself to go with the flow of my beautifully imperfect human-ness.

If it's a gorgeous day outside, I can appreciate its beauty. If the temperature is extreme, I can remember that the weather is just the weather and that it doesn't need to dictate what kind of a day I will have. There's absolutely nothing I can do about the weather, but there's a lot I can do about how I move through my day. I can shift my perspective, enjoy the day as is, and welcome joy and peace back into my life.

If someone talks about me unfairly or otherwise offends me, I can practice not taking it personally. Knowing that what they say is really about them, not me, I can let it go, knowing it will not do me one bit of good to hang onto it.

If a loved one has reached a goal, kudos to them; it's time to celebrate! If someone I love is stumbling, unable to find peace, self-esteem shattered, that's also *for* me. It's my opportunity to accept them exactly as they are, without the need to fix them. My job is simply to love them in their process.

With each situation I can consciously choose how I want to show up . . . standing for what I believe in . . . finding something to be grateful for . . . liking myself in the situation. Believing that life is always for me causes me to be optimistic and faith-filled, which is what I choose today.

~

Believing that everything in my life is for me and not against me, I take responsibility for my response to each situation and consciously choose a positive attitude.

My Life is My Ministry

I believe we all have a ministry. It's what brings our beliefs and values into our everyday lives. Our ministry gives us purpose—it's what we stand for. A call to action, our ministry reminds us that we matter in the world, that who we are makes a difference.

Our ministry is often born from adversity. We've all gone through challenges that changed us. How we look back at them sheds light on how we see ourselves today. If we focus on how we grew through each struggle, making us stronger and more resilient, they become a foundation upon which we grow through the next difficulty. One challenge at a time, we discover the depth of our own power, our own worth. Our ministry is born.

Each day offers a chance to live my ministry. Who do I choose to be in this situation? Can I stand for peace amidst chaos, acceptance instead of judgment, hopefulness as an alternative for fear and disapproval?

My work is my ministry. I can pray daily for the happiness and fulfillment of everyone I work with. Before I go into a work meeting I can get myself centered and pray for Divine Right Action, for the highest good of all concerned. My prayer lets ego/fear take a back seat to Love's highest intention.

My family, friends and loved ones are my ministry. It's so easy to find others wrong, leaving me as the only "right" one. When my loved ones are my ministry I offer them the dignity of living their own lives, while I live mine. Letting go of judgment, I pray daily for the happiness and fulfillment of every family member, my friends and loved ones, as well as those they care about.

The world is my ministry. I pray that every being knows how divinely Loved they are, and from that Love they will grow and thrive. I pray that we remember that we are all part of the same One and share the same spiritual DNA, each an integral part of life, connected at our core

My spiritual journey is my ministry. Wherever I am on my spiritual path is exactly where I'm supposed to be. Everything that looks like a misstep has been an essential stepping stone upon which the whole of my life has been built. I pray daily for my happiness and fulfillment, knowing I'm worth it.

～

My life is my ministry.
I pray daily for the highest good for all.

My Own Inner Light

Have you ever noticed how plants turn to face the sun? They instinctively know what's best for them, and they seek it. They bask in the sunlight, stretching and growing to be all they can be.

We do the same thing! In every moment, our own Truth beckons us inward as it whispers, "You are Life's grand creation. Your existence has meaning. Step into your greatness." Sometimes it's hard for me to believe that I'm truly as magnificent as my Inner Light proclaims me to be. I have dozens of reasons to think I'm not quite good enough to be an emissary of Love's graciousness upon the earth.

But then I remember that I can take charge of my thoughts today. I can decide what goes on in my mind—not my parents, my employer, my spouse or the media. I have a choice—I can either listen to all of those accumulated "I'm not good enough" beliefs, or I can plant new roots in soil that's chock-full of the faith that comes from knowing that I am God's beloved one, just as I am, even with all my human imperfections.

Knowing that there is so much more to my life than anything I've ever experienced up until this moment, I instinctively turn toward the Inner Light of my own brilliance, breathe it in and grow to be all I can be.

~

Just as plants turn toward the sun,
I turn toward the Inner Light of my own brilliance and
grow to be all I can be.

A Note from Jane

AS WE DANCE our co-creative dance with life, we get what we expect—what we believe becomes true for us. If we think life is hard, we get to be right; it will be. If we live in gratitude for what we have today with joyful expectations for tomorrow, then that will be our experience. Basking in the warmth of our own inner light shifts our attention, as well as the resulting experience.

Whenever a negative thought enters our mind, we can choose to replace it with an optimistic one, or perhaps find something to be grateful for. It takes time and practice, with an intention of being gentle with ourselves when we forget. Are you willing? I sure am! It feels good to know that in any circumstance I can choose love and I can be peace. Yes, it's work, but its good work!

It is within our power to become as cheerful, contented and successful as we make up our mind to be. The journey is one of self-discovery, nurturing a personal relationship with a God that adores us, a deeper relationship with ourselves and an expanded appreciation for our everyday life.

It's the *experience* of the dance that's important. It's the absolute knowing that we are loved unconditionally, exactly as we are, that changes us. Our outward lives become a reflection of the Divine Love that's alive in each of us, bathing us in the warmth of its light and guiding us to our greatness. We are worthy of every good thing, simply because we exist. Saying yes to the beauty of our own truth, we accept the happiness that Life offers us.

Live your life well, my friend.

With love,
Jane

About Jane Beach

For the first fifty years of her life, Jane Beach was an atheist. In a moment of awareness, she discovered that God was real; her whole life changed, and much to her surprise, she became a minister! Jane's passion is her love affair with the one she calls the Beloved. Knowing what it feels like to live in a place of unconditional love and acceptance, she is committed to creating situations for others to do the same, relaxing into their own personal relationship with the God of their understanding. As Jane says, "Once you know how Loved you are, everything else takes care of itself."

Jane's writings invite readers to investigate their own love affair with the Divine . . . their own inner beauty. Her personal relationship with life is contagious, and wherever she shows up, an atmosphere of possibility, acceptance and unconditional love abound. A retreat facilitator, Jane has written twenty-five spiritual programs that are currently being taught in classes throughout the United States, Canada, the UK, and Mexico, including the Centers for Spiritual Living, Unity, independent centers and the Institute of Noetic Sciences. Jane has recently retired as minister of the Conscious Living Center in Mountain View, California in order to take her message past its walls. She resides in Campbell, California.

You can email Jane at
revjanebeach@janebeach.com
Connect with her on Facebook at
facebook.com/RevJaneBeach
Visit Jane's author page on our website for
announcements of forthcoming books and news.

About the Publisher

Kenos Press™, a division of Six Degrees Publishing Group™, publishes literary works which are meant to encourage an intimate connection with the Divine, uplift the human spirit, and further peace by improving our universal connection with one another .

Learn more about Kenos Press™ at our link on the web at:

SixDegreesPublishing.com